PACIFIC COAST HIGHWAYS

ROAD TRIPS

This edition written and researched by

**Andrew Bender, Sara Benson, Alison Bing, Celeste Brash,
Nate Cavalieri, Adam Skolnick**

HOW TO USE THIS BOOK

Reviews

In the Destinations section:

All reviews are ordered in our authors' preference, starting with their most preferred option. Additionally:

Sights are arranged in the geographic order that we suggest you visit them and, within this order, by author preference.

Eating and Sleeping reviews are ordered by price range (budget, midrange, top end) and, within these ranges, by author preference.

Map Legend

Routes

- Trip Route
- Trip Detour
- Linked Trip
- Walk Route
- Tollway
- Freeway
- Primary
- Secondary
- Tertiary
- Lane
- Unsealed Road
- Plaza/Mall
- Steps
- ⌒ Tunnel
- Pedestrian Overpass
- Walk Track/Path

Boundaries

- International
- State/Province
- Cliff

Population

- ✪ Capital (National)
- ◉ Capital (State/Province)
- ● City/Large Town
- ● Town/Village

Transport

- ✈ Airport
- Cable Car/Funicular
- P Parking
- Train/Railway
- Tram
- Ⓜ Underground Train Station

Trips

- 1 Trip Numbers
- 9 Trip Stop
- Walking Tour
- Trip Detour

Highway Route Markers

- 97 US National Hwy
- 5 US Interstate Hwy
- 44 California State Hwy

Hydrography

- River/Creek
- Intermittent River
- Swamp/Mangrove
- Canal
- Water
- Dry/Salt/Intermittent Lake
- Glacier

Areas

- Beach
- Cemetery (Christian)
- Cemetery (Other)
- Park
- Forest
- Reservation
- Urban Area
- Sportsground

Symbols In This Book

✓ Top Tips		🍷 Food & Drink	
S Link Your Trips		🌳 Outdoors	
Tips from Locals		📷 Essential Photo	
Trip Detour		🚶 Walking Tour	
📖 History & Culture		✗ Eating	
👪 Family		🛏 Sleeping	

◉ Sights		⌷ Sleeping	
🏖 Beaches		✗ Eating	
🏃 Activities		🍷 Drinking	
🎓 Courses		☆ Entertainment	
👉 Tours		🔒 Shopping	
✦ Festivals & Events		ⓘ Information & Transport	

These symbols and abbreviations give vital information for each listing:

☎ Telephone number	☺ Pet-friendly
⊙ Opening hours	🚌 Bus
P Parking	⛴ Ferry
⊘ Nonsmoking	🚊 Tram
❄ Air-conditioning	🚆 Train
@ Internet access	apt apartments
🛜 Wi-fi access	d double rooms
🏊 Swimming pool	dm dorm beds
🥗 Vegetarian selection	q quad rooms
	r rooms
📖 English-language menu	s single rooms
	ste suites
👪 Family-friendly	tr triple rooms
	tw twin rooms

CONTENTS

PLAN YOUR TRIP

ROAD TRIPS

DESTINATIONS

CALIFORNIA DRIVING GUIDE

Bixby Bridge (p39), Big Sur

WELCOME TO
PACIFIC COAST HIGHWAYS

Starry-eyed newbies head to the Golden State to find fame and fortune, but you can do better. Come for the landscapes, stay for the farm-fresh and global fusion food, and glimpse the future in the making on America's creative coast.

The trips in this book will take you along the breezy, wildlife-rich Pacific coast highways, from the towering redwoods of Northern California, the open roads of Big Sur, through to the famed Southern Californian beaches of Orange and San Diego Counties. Take time out to explore the vineyards of Santa Barbara County, the chilled out beach cities of Monterey and Santa Cruz, and the big city lights of San Francisco and Los Angeles.

From backcountry lanes to beachside highways, we've got something for you.

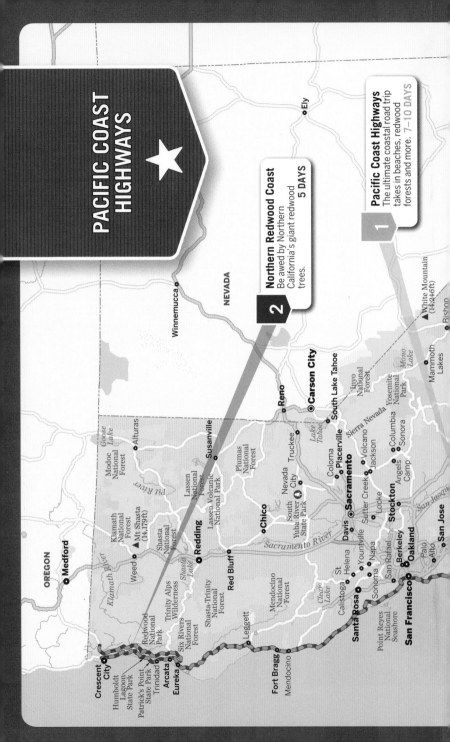

PACIFIC COAST HIGHWAYS ★

1 Pacific Coast Highways
The ultimate coastal road trip takes in beaches, redwood forests and more. 7–10 DAYS

2 Northern Redwood Coast
Be awed by Northern California's giant redwood trees. 5 DAYS

OREGON

NEVADA

Medford

Winnemucca

Ely

Carson City

Reno

South Lake Tahoe

White Mountain (14,246ft)

Bishop

Mammoth Lakes

Mono Lake

Inyo National Forest

Sierra Nevada

Yosemite National Park

Columbia Sonora

Volcano

Angels Camp

Jackson

Placerville

Coloma

Truckee

Nevada City

Lake Tahoe

Susanville

Alturas

Goose Lake

Modoc National Forest

Lassen National Forest

Plumas National Forest

Lassen Volcanic National Park

Pit River

Klamath National Forest

Mt Shasta (14,179ft)

Weed

Shasta National Forest

Klamath River

Trinity Alps Wilderness

Six Rivers National Forest

Redwood National Park

Crescent City

Humboldt Lagoon State Park

Patrick's Point State Park

Trinidad

Arcata

Eureka

Leggett

Mendocino National Forest

Shasta-Trinity National Forest

Shasta Lake

Redding

Red Bluff

Chico

South Yuba River State Park

Sacramento River

Sacramento

Davis

Locke

Sutter Creek

Stockton

San Joaquin

San Jose

Palo Alto

Oakland

Berkeley

San Francisco

San Rafael

Point Reyes National Seashore

Sonoma

Napa

Yountville

St Helena

Calistoga

Santa Rosa

Clear Lake

Fort Bragg

Mendocino

ARIZONA

Kingman

Lake Havasu City

Goffs

Needles

Las Vegas

Beatty

Tecopa

Mojave National Preserve

Amboy

Baker

Furnace Creek

Death Valley National Park

Stovepipe Wells Village

Mt Whitney (14,505ft) ▲

Panamint Springs

Telescope Peak (11,049ft)

Kings Canyon National Park

Sierra National Forest

Sequoia National Park

Sequoia National Forest

Barstow

Mojave Desert

Victorville

San Bernardino

Joshua Tree National Park

Indio

Palm Springs

Anza-Borrego Desert State Park

Salton Sea

Mexicali

Blythe

Yuma

MEXICO

Fresno

Bakersfield

Mojave

Kern River

Kings River

Pasadena

Los Angeles

Anaheim

Seal Beach

Long Beach

Malibu

Santa Monica

Huntington Beach

Newport Beach

Laguna Beach

San Clemente

Oceanside

La Jolla

San Diego

Cleveland National Forest

Tijuana

Pinnacles National Monument

Paso Robles

San Luis Obispo

Los Olivos

Buellton Solvang

Lompoc

Santa Barbara

Ventana Wilderness

Big Sur

Morro Bay

Pismo Beach

Channel Islands

Catalina Island

San Clemente Island

San Nicolas Island

Santa Cruz

Monterey

3

Big Sur
Stunning ocean vistas beckon along this stretch of highway.
2 DAYS

4

Disneyland & Orange County Beaches
Meet Mickey Mouse, then surf the 'OC' Coast.   **2–4 DAYS**

PACIFIC OCEAN

0 — 100 km
0 — 50 miles

N

PACIFIC COAST
HIGHWAYS
HIGHLIGHTS
★

Golden Gate Bridge (left) Get another perspective on this world-famous, 20th-century engineering feat by driving across it.
See it on Trip 1

Redwood Coast (above) Nothing compares to the awe you'll feel while walking underneath these ancient trees.
See it on Trips 1 2

SoCal Beaches (right) Enjoy your ultimate beach vacation on the warm sands of Orange and San Diego Counties.
See them on Trips 1 4

Victorian architecture, San Francisco

SAN FRANCISCO

Ride the clanging cable cars up unbelievably steep hills, snake down Lombard St's famous hairpin turns, cruise through Golden Gate Park and drive across the arching Golden Gate Bridge. Then go get lost in the creatively offbeat neighborhoods of California's capital of weird.

Getting Around

Avoid driving downtown. Cable cars are slow and scenic (single rides $6). MUNI streetcar and bus are faster but infrequent after 9pm (fares $2). BART (tickets from $1.75) run high-speed Bay Area trains. Taxis cost $2.75 per mile; meters start at $3.50.

Parking

Street parking is scarce and meter readers ruthless. Meters take coins, sometimes credit cards; central pay stations accept coins or cards. Overnight hotel parking averages $35 to $50; downtown parking garages start at $2.50 per hour or $25 per day.

Where to Eat

The Ferry Building, Mission District and South of Market (SoMa) are foodie faves. Don't miss the city's outdoor farmers markets either. Head to North Beach for Italian, Chinatown for dim sum, the Mission District for Mexican, and the Sunset or Richmond for pan-Asian.

Where to Stay

The Marina is near the family-friendly waterfront and Fisherman's Wharf. Downtown and Union Square are more expensive, but conveniently located for walking. Avoid the rough-edged Civic Center and Tenderloin neighborhoods.

Useful Websites

San Francisco Travel (www.sanfrancisco.travel) Destination info, events calendar and accommodations bookings.

SF Station (www.sfstation.com) Nightlife, restaurants, shopping and the arts.

Lonely Planet (www.lonelyplanet.com/usa/san-francisco) Travel tips and travelers' forums.

Road Trip through San Francisco: 1

Destinations coverage: p54

Los Angeles skyline

LOS ANGELES

Loony LA, land of starstruck dreams and Hollywood Tinseltown magic. You may think you know what to expect: celebrity worship, Botoxed beach blondes, endless traffic and earthquakes. But it's also California's most ethnically diverse city, with new immigrants arriving daily, evolving the boundary-breaking global arts, music and food scenes.

Getting Around

Angelenos drive everywhere. Freeway traffic jams are endless, but worst during morning and afternoon rush hours. Metro operates buses and subway and light-rail trains (fares $1.75), with limited night and weekend services. DASH minibuses (single-ride 50¢) zip around downtown; Santa Monica's Big Blue Bus (fares from $1) connects West LA. Taxis cost $2.80 per mile; meters start at $2.85.

Parking

Street parking is tough. Meters take coins, sometimes credit cards; central pay stations accept coins or cards. Valet parking is ubiquitous, typically $5 to $10 plus tip. Overnight hotel parking averages $25 to $40.

Where to Eat

Food trucks are a local obsession. Downtown cooks up a worldly mix, with Little Tokyo, Chinatown, Thai Town, Koreatown and Latin-flavored East LA nearby. Trend-setting eateries inhabit Hollywood, Mid-City, Santa Monica and Venice.

Where to Stay

For beach life, escape to Santa Monica or Venice. Long Beach is convenient to Disneyland and Orange County. Party people adore Hollywood; culture vultures, Downtown LA.

Useful Websites

LA Inc (http://discoverlosangeles.com) City's official tourism website.

LA Weekly (www.laweekly.com) Arts, entertainment, dining and events calendar.

Lonely Planet (www.lonelyplanet.com/usa/los-angeles) Travel tips, hotel reservations and travelers' forums.

Road Trip through Los Angeles: 1
Destinations coverage: p90

NEED ^{TO} KNOW

Climate

Arcata
GO Apr–Oct

San Francisco
GO Apr–Oct

Yosemite Village
GO Apr–Oct

Los Angeles
GO Apr–Oct

Palm Springs
GO Dec–Apr

Desert, dry climate
Dry climate
Warm to hot summers, mild winters
Warm to hot summers, cold winters

When to Go

High Season (Jun–Aug)

» Accommodations prices up 50% to 100%.

» Major holidays are even busier and more expensive.

» Summer is low season in the desert: temperatures exceed 100°F (38°C).

Shoulder Season (Apr–May & Sep–Oct)

» Crowds and prices drop, especially along the coast and in the mountains.

» Typically wetter in spring, drier in autumn.

» Milder temperatures and sunny, cloudless days.

Low Season (Nov–Mar)

» Accommodations rates drop in cities and by the coast.

» Many attractions open fewer days and shorter hours.

» Chilly temperatures and rainstorms; mudslides occasionally wash out coastal highways.

» In the mountains, carry tire chains; heavy snowfall closes higher-elevation roads.

» Winter is peak season in SoCal's desert regions.

Daily Costs

Budget: less than $75

» Camping: $20–40

» Meals in roadside diners and cafes: $10–20

» Graze farmers markets for cheaper eats

» Hit the beach and find 'free days' at museums

Midrange: $75–200

» Two-star motel or hotel double room: $75–150

» Meals in casual and midrange restaurants: $20–40

» Theme-park admission: $40–100

Top end: over $200

» Three-star lodging: from $150 per night in high season, more for ocean views

» Three-course meal in top restaurant: $75 plus wine

Eating

Roadside diners & cafes
Cheap and simple; abundant only outside cities.

Beach shacks Casual burgers, shakes and seafood meals with ocean views.

National, state & theme parks Mostly so-so, overpriced cafeteria-style or deli picnic fare.

Vegetarians Food restrictions and allergies can usually be catered for at restaurants.

Eating price indicators represent the average cost of a main dish:

$	less than $10
$$	$10–$20
$$$	more than $20

Sleeping

Motels & hotels Ubiquitous along well-trafficked highways and in major tourist areas.

Camping & cabins Ranging from rustic campsites to luxury 'glamping' resorts.

B&Bs Quaint, romantic and pricey inns, found in most coastal and mountain towns.

Hostels Cheap and basic, but almost exclusively in cities.

Price indicators represent the average cost of a double room with private bathroom:

$	less than $100
$$	$100–$200
$$$	more than $200

Arriving in California

Los Angeles International Airport

Rental cars Major companies offer shuttles to off-airport lots.

Door-to-door shared-ride shuttles $16 to $27 one-way (reservations recommended).

Taxis $30 to $50 to Santa Monica, Hollywood or Downtown; 30 minutes to one hour.

Buses Take Shuttle C (free) to LAX City Bus Center or Metro FlyAway bus ($8) to Downtown LA.

San Francisco International Airport

Rental cars Take free AirTrain blue line to SFO Rental Car Center.

Door-to-door shared-ride shuttles $15 to $18 one-way (reservations recommended).

Taxis $35 to $50 plus tip to most San Francisco neighborhoods; 30 to 50 minutes.

Train BART ($8.25, 30 minutes to downtown SF) leaves every 20 minutes (take free AirTrain from any terminal to BART station).

Money

ATMs are widely available. Credit cards are accepted almost universally.

Tipping

Tipping is expected. Standard tips: 18% to 20% in restaurants; 15% for taxis; $1 per drink in bars; $2 per bag for porters.

Opening Hours

Banks 8:30am–4:30pm Mon–Fri, some to 5:30pm Fri, 9am–12:30pm Sat

Business hours (general) 9am–5pm Mon–Fri

Post offices 9am–5pm Mon–Fri, some 9am–noon Sat

Restaurants 7am–10:30am, 11:30am–2:30pm & 5–9:30pm daily, some later Fri & Sat

Shops 10am–6pm Mon-Sat, noon–5pm Sun (malls open later)

Useful Websites

Lonely Planet (www.lonelyplanet.com/usa/california) Destination info, hotel bookings, travelers' forums and more.

California Travel and Tourism Commission (www.visitcalifornia.com) Multilingual trip-planning guides and an events calendar.

For more, see Driving in California (p114)

Road Trips

Highway 1, Big Sur (p37)
HAUKE DRESSLER / ROBERT HARDING ©

Pacific Coast Highways

Our top pick for classic California dreamin' snakes along the Pacific coast for 1000 miles. Uncover beaches, seafood shacks and piers for catching sunsets over boundless ocean horizons.

TRIP HIGHLIGHTS

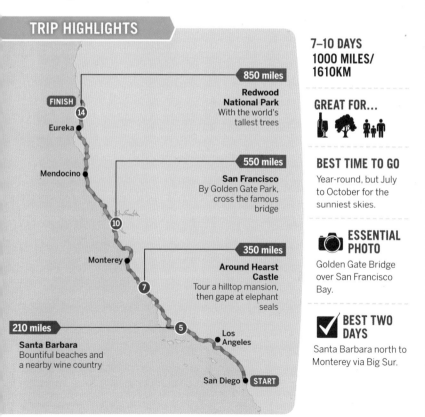

850 miles

Redwood National Park
With the world's tallest trees

550 miles

San Francisco
By Golden Gate Park, cross the famous bridge

350 miles

Around Hearst Castle
Tour a hilltop mansion, then gape at elephant seals

210 miles

Santa Barbara
Bountiful beaches and a nearby wine country

FINISH

Eureka

Mendocino

Monterey

Los Angeles

San Diego · START

7–10 DAYS
1000 MILES/ 1610KM

GREAT FOR...

BEST TIME TO GO
Year-round, but July to October for the sunniest skies.

ESSENTIAL PHOTO
Golden Gate Bridge over San Francisco Bay.

BEST TWO DAYS
Santa Barbara north to Monterey via Big Sur.

1 Pacific Coast Highways

Make your escape from California's tangled, traffic-jammed freeways and cruise in the slow lane. Once you get rolling, it'll be almost painful to leave the ocean behind for too long. Officially, only the short, sun-loving stretch of Hwy 1 through Orange and Los Angeles Counties can legally call itself Pacific Coast Highway (PCH). But never mind those technicalities, because equally bewitching ribbons of Hwy 1 and Hwy 101 await all along this route.

FINISH Crescent City
14 Redwood National Park
2
Arcata
13 Eureka
Fortuna
Redding
Red Bluff
Leggett
Mendocino & Fort Bragg
12
Willits
Around Point Arena
11
Clearlake
Santa Rosa
Bodega Bay
Fairfield
Point Reyes National Seashore p24
Oakland
San Francisco 10
San Jose
Santa Cruz
Monterey

PACIFIC OCEAN

0 ————— 100 km
0 ————— 50 miles

❶ San Diego (p106)

Begin at the bottom of the state map, where the pretty peninsular beach town of **Coronado** is connected to the San Diego mainland by the white-sand beaches of the **Silver Strand**. If you've seen Marilyn Monroe cavort in *Some Like It Hot,* you'll recognize the **Hotel Del Coronado** (☎800-582-2595, 619-435-6611; www.hoteldel. com; 1500 Orange Ave), which has hosted US presidents, celebrities and royalty, including the Prince of Wales who gave up his throne to marry a Coronado divorcée. Wander the turreted palace's labyrinthine corridors, then quaff tropical cocktails at ocean-view Babcock & Story Bar.

Be thrilled by driving over the 2.1-mile-long **Coronado Bay Bridge**. Detour inland to Balboa Park. Head west, then south to Point Loma's **Cabrillo National Monument** (www.nps.gov/ cabr; per car $5; ◷9am-5pm, last entry 4:30pm; 🅿) for captivating bay

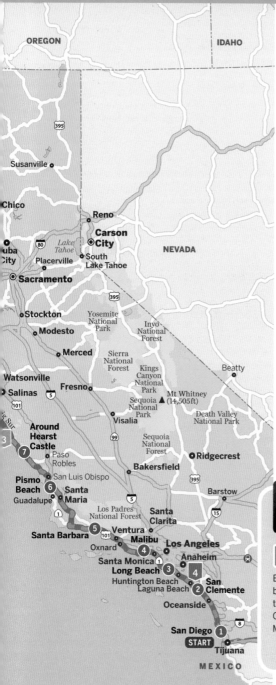

panoramas from the 19th-century lighthouse and monument to the West Coast's first Spanish explorers. Rolling north of **Mission Beach**, where an old-fashioned amusement park is dwarfed by SeaWorld, suddenly you're in hoity-toity **La Jolla**, beyond which lie North County's beach towns.

The Drive » It's a 50-mile trip from La Jolla north along coastal roads then the I-5 into Orange County (aka the 'OC'), passing Camp Pendleton Marine Corps Base and buxom-shaped San Onofre Nuclear Generating Station. Exit at San Clemente and follow Avenida del Mar downhill to the beach.

❷ San Clemente

Life behind the conservative 'Orange Curtain' is far different than in most other laid-back, liberal California beach towns. Apart from glamorous beaches where famous TV shows and movies

LINK YOUR TRIP

Big Sur
3 Get lost on the rugged Big Sur coast, stretched between Hearst Castle and the painterly scenery of Carmel-by-the-Sea on the Monterey Peninsula.

19

have been filmed, you can still uncover the California beach culture of yesteryear here in off-the-beaten-path spots like San Clemente. Home to living surfing legends, top-notch surfboard companies and *Surfer* magazine, this may be the last place in the OC where you can authentically live the surf lifestyle. Ride your own board or swim at the city's main beach beside San Clemente Pier. A fast detour inland, the community's **Surfing Heritage Foundation** (www.surfingheritage.com; 101 Calle Iglesia; admission by donation; ☺11am-5pm) exhibits surfboards ridden by the greats, from Duke Kahanamoku to Kelly Slater.

The Drive ›› Slingshot north on I-5, exiting onto Hwy 1 near Dana Point. Speed by the wealthy artists colony of Laguna Beach, wild Crystal Cove State Park, Newport Beach's yacht harbor and 'Surf City USA' Huntington Beach (p104). Turn west off Hwy 1 near Naples toward Long Beach, about 45 miles from San Clemente.

❸ Long Beach

In Long Beach, the biggest stars are the **Queen Mary** (www.queenmary.com; 1126 Queens Hwy; adult/child from $25/14; ☺10am-6pm Mon-Thu, to 7pm Fri-Sun), a grand (and allegedly haunted) British ocean liner permanently moored here, and the giant **Aquarium of the Pacific** (www.aquariumofpacific.org; 100 Aquarium Way; adult/child $29/15; ☺9am-6pm; 🚻); a high-tech romp through an underwater world in which sharks dart and jellyfish float. Often overlooked, the **Long Beach Museum of Art** (www.lbma.org; 2300 E Ocean Blvd; adult/child $7/free; ☺11am-5pm Fri-Sun, to 8pm Thu) focuses on California modernism and contemporary mixed-media inside a 20th-century mansion by the ocean, while the urban **Museum of Latin American Art** (www.molaa.org; 628 Alamitos Ave; adult/child $7/free; ☺11am-5pm Wed & Fri-Sun, to 9pm Thu)

shows off contemporary south-of-the-border art.

The Drive ›› Wind slowly around the ruggedly scenic Palos Verdes Peninsula. Follow Hwy 1 north past the South Bay's primetime beaches. Curving around LAX airport and Marina del Rey, Hwy 1 continues north to Venice (see p93), Santa Monica (see p93) and all the way to Malibu, over 50 miles from Long Beach.

❹ Malibu (p91)

Leaving traffic-jammed LA behind, Hwy 1 breezes northwest of Santa Monica to Malibu. You'll feel like a movie star walking around on the public beaches, backing against gated compounds owned by Hollywood celebs. One mansion you can actually get a look inside is the **Getty Villa** (www.getty.edu; 17985 Pacific Coast Hwy; per car $10, parking reservation required; ☺10am-5pm Wed-Mon), a hilltop showcase of Greek, Roman and Etruscan antiquities and manicured gardens. Next to Malibu Lagoon State Beach, west of the surfers by Malibu Pier, **Adamson House** (www.adamsonhouse.org; 23200 Pacific Coast Hwy; adult/child $7/2; ☺11am-3pm Wed-Sat, last tour 2pm) is a Spanish-Moorish villa lavishly decorated with locally made hand-painted tiles. Motoring further west along the coast, where the Santa Monica Mountains plunge into

TROUBLE-FREE ROAD TRIPPING

In coastal areas, thick fog may impede driving – slow down and if it's too soupy, get off the road. Along coastal cliffs, watch out for falling rocks and mudslides that could damage or disable your car if struck. For current highway conditions, including road closures (which aren't uncommon during the rainy winter season) and construction updates, call ☎800-427-7623 or visit www.dot.ca.gov.

the sea, take time out for a frolic on Malibu's mega-popular beaches like sandy Point Dume, Zuma or Leo Carrillo.

The Drive » Hwy 1 crosses into Ventura County, winding alongside the ocean and windy Point Mugu. In Oxnard, join Hwy 101 northbound beyond Ventura, a jumping-off point for boat trips to Channel Islands, to Santa Barbara, just over 70 miles from Malibu Pier.

TRIP HIGHLIGHT

❺ Santa Barbara (p82)

Seaside Santa Barbara has almost perfect weather and a string of idyllic beaches, where surfers, kite flyers, dog walkers and surfers mingle. Get a close-up of the city's iconic Mediterranean-style architecture along **State St** downtown or from the **county courthouse** (www. santabarbaracourthouse.org; 1100 Anacapa St; admission free; ⏰8:30am-4:35pm Mon-Fri, 10am-4:35pm Sat & Sun), its tower rising above the red-tiled rooftops. Gaze south toward the busy harborfront and **Stearns Wharf** (www.stearnswharf. org; 🚻) or north to the historic Spanish mission church (see p82). Santa Barbara's balmy climate is also perfect for growing grapes. A 45-minute drive northwest along Hwy 154, visit the

Mission Santa Barbara (p82)

Santa Ynez Valley wine country (see p87), made famous by the 2004 movie *Sideways*. Hit wine-tasting rooms in **Los Olivos** (p88), then take Foxen Canyon Rd north past more wineries to rejoin Hwy 101.

The Drive » Keep following fast Hwy 101 northbound or detour west onto slow Hwy 1, which squiggles along the Pacific coastline past Guadalupe, gateway to North America's largest sand dunes. Both highways meet up again in Pismo Beach, 100 miles northwest of Santa Barbara.

❻ Pismo Beach

A classic California beach town, Pismo Beach has a long, lazy stretch of sand for swimming, surfing and strolling out onto the pier at sunset. After digging into bowls of clam chowder and baskets of fried seafood at surf-casual cafes, check out the retro family fun at the bowling alley, billiards halls and bars uphill from the beach, or dash 10 miles up Hwy 101 to the vintage **Sunset Drive-In** (www.fairoakstheatre.net; 255 Elks Lane, San Luis Obispo; 🚻), where you can put your feet up on the dash and munch on bottomless bags of popcorn while watching Hollywood blockbuster double-features.

The Drive » Follow Hwy 101 north past San Luis Obispo, exiting onto Hwy 1 west to landmark Morro Rock in Morro Bay. North of Cayucos, Hwy 1 rolls through bucolic pasture lands, only swinging back to

LOCAL KNOWLEDGE
AMY STARBIN, LA SCREENWRITER & MOM

For a fun way to cool off when driving through LA along the coast, bring the family out to **Santa Monica Pier** (www.santamonicapier. org). Not only do you get a great view of the ocean, you can also get up close and personal with sea life at the **aquarium** (www.healthebay.org). Then head up top for a spin on the carousel used in *The Sting* or the solar-powered Ferris wheel.

Top: Pacific Park, Santa Monica Pier
Left: Monterey Bay Aquarium (p24)
Right: Pool, Hearst Castle

the coast at Cambria. Ten miles further north stands Hearst Castle, about 60 miles from Pismo Beach.

---

❼ Around Hearst Castle

Hilltop **Hearst Castle** (📞info 805-927-2020, reservations 800-444-4445; www.hearstcastle.org; tours adult/child from $25/12; ⊙daily, call for hr) is California's most famous monument to wealth and ambition. William Randolph Hearst, the early-20th-century newspaper magnate, entertained Hollywood stars and royalty at this fantasy estate furnished with European antiques, accented by shimmering pools and surrounded by flowering gardens. Try to make tour reservations in advance, especially for living-history evening programs during the Christmas holiday season.

About 4.5 miles further north along Hwy 1, park at the signposted vista point and amble the boardwalk to view the enormous **elephant seal colony** that breeds, molts, sleeps, plays and fights on the beach. Seals haul out year-round, but the winter birthing and mating season peaks on Valentine's Day. Nearby, **Piedras Blancas Light Station** (www. piedrasblancas.org; tour adult/ child $10/5; ⊙call for hr) is

23

DETOUR: POINT REYES

Start: ⑩ San Francisco

A rough-hewn beauty, **Point Reyes National Seashore** (www.nps.gov/pore; admission free; ☉sunrise-midnight; 🚻) lures marine mammals and birds, as well as scores of shipwrecks. It was here that Sir Francis Drake repaired his ship the *Golden Hind* in 1579 and, while he was at it, claimed the indigenous land for England. Follow Sir Francis Drake Blvd west out to the point's edge-of-the-world lighthouse, whipped by ferocious winds, where you can observe migrating whales in winter. The lighthouse is about 10 miles west of Point Reyes Station off Hwy 1 along the Marin County coast.

an outstandingly scenic spot.

The Drive » Fill your car's gas tank before plunging north into the redwood forests of the remote Big Sur coast (see p37), where precipitous cliffs dominate the seascape, and tourist services are few and far between. Hwy 1 keeps curving north to the Monterey Peninsula, approximately a three-hour, 100-mile trip from Hearst Castle.

⑧ Monterey (p77)

As Big Sur loosens its condor's talons on the coastal highway, Hwy 1 rolls gently downhill towards Monterey Bay. The fishing community of Monterey is the heart of Steinbeck country, and although Cannery Row today is touristy claptrap, it's worth strolling down to step inside the mesmerizing

Monterey Bay Aquarium (📞tickets 866-963-9645; www.montereybayaquarium. org; 886 Cannery Row; adult/child $40/25; ☉10am-5pm or 6pm daily, extended summer hr; 📶🚻), inhabiting a converted sardine cannery on the shores of a national marine sanctuary. All kinds of aquatic denizens swim in giant tanks here, from sea stars to pot-bellied seahorses and comical sea otters.

The Drive » It's a relatively quick 45-mile trip north to Santa Cruz. Hwy 1 traces the crescent shoreline of Monterey Bay, passing Elkhorn Slough wildlife refuge near Moss Landing boat harbor, Watsonville's strawberry and artichoke farms, and a string of tiny beach towns in Santa Cruz County.

⑨ Santa Cruz (p74)

Here, the flower power of the 1960s lives on,

and bumper stickers on surfboard-laden woodies shout, 'Keep Santa Cruz weird.' Next to the ocean, **Santa Cruz Beach Boardwalk** (📞831-423-5590; www. beachboardwalk.com; 400 Beach St; admission free, rides $3-6; ☉seasonal schedules vary, call for hr; 🚻) has a glorious old-school Americana vibe and a 1911 Looff carousel. Its fun-for-all atmosphere is punctuated by squeals from nervous nellies on the stomach-turning Giant Dipper, a 1920s wooden roller coaster that's a national historic landmark, as seen in the vampire cult-classic movie *The Lost Boys*.

A kitschy, old-fashioned tourist trap, the **Mystery Spot** (📞831-423-8897; www. mysteryspot.com; 465 Mystery Spot Rd; admission $6, parking $5; ☉daily, hr vary; 🚻) makes compasses point crazily, while mysterious forces push you around and buildings lean at odd angles; call for directions, opening hours and tour reservations.

The Drive » It's a blissful 75-mile coastal run from Santa Cruz up to San Francisco past Pescadero, Half Moon Bay and Pacifica, where Hwy 1 encounters washout-prone Devil's Slide. Merge with heavy freeway traffic in Daly City, staying on Hwy 1 north through the city into Golden Gate Park.

⑩ San Francisco (p54)

Gridlock may shock your system after hundreds of lazy miles of wide-open, rolling coast. But don't despair. Hwy 1 runs straight through the city's biggest, most breathable greenspace: **Golden Gate Park** (www. golden-gate-park.com; admission free; 🚶🐾). You could easily spend all day in the conservatory of flowers, arboretum and botanical gardens, perusing the **California Academy of Sciences** (www.calacademy.org; 55 Music Concourse Dr; adult/child $35/25; ⏰9:30am-5pm Mon-Sat, 11am-5pm Sun; 🚶) and the **de Young Museum** (www.famsf.org/ deyoung; 50 Hagiwara Tea Garden Dr; adult/child $10/ free; ⏰9:30am-5:15pm Tue-Sun) of fine arts. (For our self-guided walking tour of San Francisco, see p64). Then follow Hwy 1 north over the **Golden Gate Bridge**. Guarding the entry to San Francisco Bay, this iconic bridge is named after the straits it spans, not for its 'International Orange' paint job. Park in the lot on the bridge's south or north side, then traipse out onto the pedestrian walkway for a photo.

The Drive ≫ Past Sausalito, leave Hwy 101 in Marin City for slow-moving, wonderfully twisted Hwy 1 along the Marin County coast. Over the next 210 miles to Mendocino via Bodega Bay, revel in a remarkably uninterrupted stretch of coastal highway. Just over halfway along, watch for the lighthouse road turnoff north of Point Arena town.

⑪ Around Point Arena

The fishing fleets of Bodega Bay and Jenner's harbor-seal colony are the last things you'll see before PCH dives into California's great rural northlands. Hwy 1 twists and turns past the Sonoma Coast's state parks packed with hiking trails, sand dunes and beaches, as well as underwater marine reserves, rhododendron groves and a 19th-century, Russian fur-trading fort. At Sea Ranch, don't let exclusive-looking vacation homes prevent you from following public-access trailhead signs and staircases down to empty beaches and across ocean bluffs. Further north, guarding an unbelievably windy point since 1908, **Point Arena Lighthouse** (www.pointarenalighthouse. com; 45500 Lighthouse Rd; adult/child $7.50/1; ⏰10am-3:30pm, to 4:30pm late May-early Sep; 🚶) is the only lighthouse in California where you can actually climb to the top. Check in at the museum, then ascend the 115ft tower to inspect the Fresnel lens and panoramas of the sea and the jagged San Andreas Fault below.

The Drive ≫ It's an hour-long, 35-mile drive north along Hwy 1 from the Point Arena Lighthouse turnoff to Mendocino, crossing the Navarro, Little and Big Rivers. Feel free to stop and stretch at wind-tossed state beaches, parklands criss-crossed by hiking trails and tiny coastal towns along the way.

🗨 LOCAL KNOWLEDGE: GRIZZLY CREEK REDWOODS STATE PARK

To find the best hidden redwood groves, **Grizzly Creek Redwoods State Park** (www.parks.ca.gov; per car $8; ⏰sunrise-sunset; 🚶) is the place to go. It's smaller than other parks, but so out of the way that it's pristine. Head to Cheatham Grove for lush sorrel carpets under the trees, then take a dip in summer swimming holes along the Van Duzen River. Bonus factoid: *Return of the Jedi* scenes were shot here. North of the Avenue of the Giants, exit Hwy 101 onto Hwy 36, then drive east for 17 miles.

Richard Stenger, retired park ranger

⑫ Mendocino (p66) & Fort Bragg (p68)

Looking more like Cape Cod than California, the quaint maritime town of **Mendocino** has white picket fences surrounding New England–style cottages with blooming gardens and redwood-built water towers. Its dramatic headlands jutting into the Pacific, this yesteryear timber town and shipping port was 'discovered' by artists and bohemians in the 1950s and has served as a scenic backdrop in over 50 movies. Once you've browsed the souvenir shops and art galleries selling everything from driftwood carvings to homemade fruit jams, escape north to workaday **Fort Bragg**, with its simple fishing harbor and brewpub, stopping first for a short hike on the ecological staircase and pygmy forest trail at oceanfront **Jug Handle State Natural Reserve** (www.parks. ca.gov; Hwy 1; admission free; ☉ sunrise-sunset; 👥).

The Drive » About 25 miles north of Mendocino, Westport is the last hamlet along this rugged stretch of Hwy 1. Rejoin Hwy 101 northbound at Leggett

for another 90 miles to Eureka, detouring along the Avenue of the Giants and, if you have more time to spare, to the Lost Coast.

⑬ Eureka (p69)

Hwy 101 trundles alongside **Humboldt Bay National Wildlife Refuge** (www.fws.gov/humboldtbay), a major stopover for migratory birds on the Pacific Flyway. Next comes the sleepy railroad town of Eureka. As you wander downtown, check the ornate **Carson Mansion** (143 M St), built in the 1880s by a timber baron and adorned with dizzying Victorian turrets, towers, gables and gingerbread details. Also a historical park, **Blue Ox Millworks** (www.blueoxmill.com; 1 X St; self-guided tour adult/child $10/5; ☉9am-4pm Mon-Sat) still creates Victorian detailing by hand using traditional carpentry and 19th-century equipment. Back by Eureka's harborfront, climb aboard the blue-and-white **1910 Madaket** (☎707-445-1910; www. humboldtbaymaritimemuseum. com; foot of C St; adult/child $18/10; ☉mid-May–early Oct, call for hr). Sunset cocktail cruises serve

from California's smallest licensed bar.

The Drive » Follow Hwy 101 north past the Rastafarian-hippie college town of Arcata and turnoffs for Trinidad State Beach and Patrick's Point State Park. Hwy 101 drops out of the trees beside marshy Humboldt Lagoons State Park, rolling north towards Orick, just over 40 miles from Eureka.

TRIP HIGHLIGHT

⑭ Redwood National Park (p72)

At last, you'll reach **Redwood National Park** (www.nps.gov/redw, www. parks.ca.gov; state park day-use per car $8; 👥). Get oriented to the tallest trees on earth at the coastal **Kuchel Visitor Center** (☉9am-5pm, to 4pm Nov-Feb; 👥), just south of Orick. Then commune with the coastal giants on their own mossy turf inside **Lady Bird Johnson Grove** or the majestic **Tall Trees Grove** (free drive-and-hike permit required). For more untouched redwood forests, wind along the 8-mile **Newton B Drury Scenic Parkway**, passing grassy meadows where Roosevelt elk roam, then follow Trip 2 all the way north to Crescent City, the last pit-stop before the Oregon border.

Right Mendocino coast

STEPHEN SAKS / GETTY IMAGES ©

Northern Redwood Coast

2

Hug a 700-year-old tree, stroll moody coastal bluffs and drop in on roadside attractions of yesteryear on this trip through verdant redwood parks and personality-packed villages.

TRIP HIGHLIGHTS

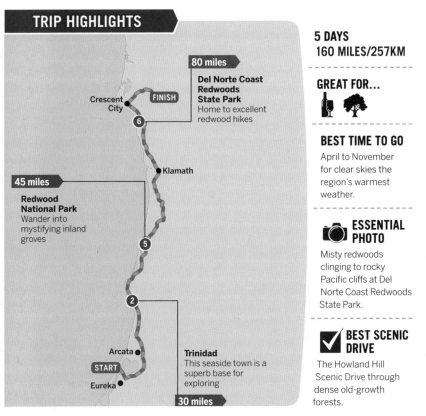

80 miles

Del Norte Coast Redwoods State Park
Home to excellent redwood hikes

FINISH

Crescent City

6

Klamath

45 miles

Redwood National Park
Wander into mystifying inland groves

5

2

Arcata

START

Eureka

Trinidad
This seaside town is a superb base for exploring

30 miles

5 DAYS
160 MILES/257KM

GREAT FOR...

BEST TIME TO GO
April to November for clear skies the region's warmest weather.

ESSENTIAL PHOTO
Misty redwoods clinging to rocky Pacific cliffs at Del Norte Coast Redwoods State Park.

BEST SCENIC DRIVE
The Howland Hill Scenic Drive through dense old-growth forests.

Left Humboldt Redwoods State Park

2 Northern Redwood Coast

This trip may have been charted in the glory days of the midcentury American road trip – roadside attractions include giant Paul Bunyan statues, drive-through trees and greasy burger stands – but that might as well be yesterday in this land of towering, mystical, ancient redwood forests. Curving roads and misty trails bring visitors to lush, spectacular natural wonders that are unlike any other place on earth.

① Samoa Peninsula

Even though this trip is about misty primeval forest, the beginning is a study of opposites: the grassy dunes and windswept beaches of the 7-mile long **Samoa Peninsula**.

At the peninsula's south end is **Samoa Dunes Recreation Area** (☉sunrise-sunset), part of a 34-mile-long dune system that's the largest in Northern California. While it's great for picnicking or fishing, the wildlife viewing is excellent. You might see 200 species of migrating waterfowl in spring and fall, songbirds in spring and summer, shorebirds in fall and winter, and waders year-round. Or,

leave the landlubbers behind and take a **Harbor Cruise** (www. humboldtbaymaritimemuseum. com; 75-minute narrated cruise adult/child $18/10, cocktail cruise $10) aboard the 1910 *Madaket,* America's oldest continuously operating passenger vessel. Leaving from the foot of C St, it ferried mill workers before the Samoa Bridge was built in 1972. The $10 sunset cocktail cruise serves drinks from the smallest licensed bar in the state.

The Drive » Head north on Hwy 101 passing myriad views of Humboldt Bay. Pass Arcata and take the exit to Trinidad. Note that the corridor between Eureka (p69) and Arcata is a closely watched safety corridor (aka speed trap), so keep it slow.

TRIP HIGHLIGHT

② Trinidad (p70)

Perched on an ocean bluff, cheery Trinidad somehow manages an off-the-beaten-path feel despite a constant flow of visitors. The free town map at the information kiosk will help you navigate the town's cute little shops and several fantastic hiking trails, most notably the **Trinidad Head Trail** with superb coastal views; excellent for whale-watching (December to April). If the weather is nice, stroll the exceptionally beautiful cove at **Trinidad State Beach**; if not, make for the **HSU Telonicher Marine Laboratory** (☎707-826-3671; www.

humboldt.edu/marinelab; Ewing St; ⏰9am-4:30pm Mon-Fri, 10am-5pm Sat & Sun Sep–mid-May; 🚹). It has a touch tank, several aquariums (look for the giant Pacific octopus), an enormous whale jaw and a cool three-dimensional map of the ocean floor. You can also join a naturalist on tidepooling expeditions (90 minutes, $3); call ahead to ask about conditions.

The Drive » Head back north on Patrick's Point drive to hug the shore for 6 miles.

- - - - - - - - - - - -

❸ Patrick's Point State Park (p71)

Coastal bluffs jut out to sea at 640-acre **Patrick's Point State Park** (📞707-677-3570; 4150 Patrick's Point Dr; day use $8; 🚹), where sandy beaches abut rocky headlands. The super-easy access to dramatic

🔗 LINK YOUR TRIP

1 Pacific Coast Highways

Head south on *the* classic west-coast road trip, following the Pacific for 1000 glorious miles though small-time coastal towns and the urban hubs of San Francisco, Los Angeles and San Diego.

GIANT TREES

With lots of kitsch mid-century appeal, the following destinations are a throwback to those bygone days of the great American road trip.

Trees of Mystery (www.treesofmystery.net; 15500 Hwy 101; adult/child & senior $15/8; ⊙8am-7pm Jun-Sep, 9am-5.30pm Sep-May; 🛈) It's hard to miss the giant statues of Paul Bunyan and Babe the Blue Ox towering over the parking lot at this shameless, if lovable, tourist trap. It has gondola running through the redwood canopy and, if you come on summer weekends, the lumberjack giant even cracks wise at tourists wandering in from the parking lot.

Chandelier Drive Thru Tree (www.drivethrutree.com; 67402 Drive Thru Tree Road, Leggett; $5 per car, ⊙8:30am-dusk; 🛈) Fold in your mirrors and inch forward, then cool off in the überkitsch gift shop.

Shrine Drive-Thru Tree ($3/6 walk/drive through; 13078 Avenue of the Giants, Myers Flat; ⊙sunrise-sunset; 🛈) Look up to the sky as you roll through, on the Ave of the Giants in Myers Flat. Though it's the least impressive of the three, it's a necessary stop for the drive-through trifecta.

Tour-Thru Tree (430 Highway 169, Klamath; ⊙sunrise-sunset; 🛈) Squeeze through a tree and check out an emu.

coastal bluffs makes this a best bet for families, but any age will find a feast for the senses as they climb rock formations, search for breaching whales, carefully navigate tidepools and listen to barking sea lions and singing birds. The park also has **Sumêg**, an authentic reproduction of a Yurok village, with hand-hewn redwood buildings. In the native plant garden you'll find species for making traditional baskets and medicines. The 2-mile **Rim Trail,** a former Yurok trail around the bluffs, circles the point with access to huge rocky outcrops. Don't miss **Wedding Rock,** one of the park's most romantic spots, or **Agate Beach** where lucky

visitors find bits of jade and sea-polished agate.

The Drive » Make your way back out to Hwy 101 through thick stands of redwoods. North another 5 minutes will bring you to the sudden clearing of Big Lagoon, part of Humboldt Lagoons State Park. Continue just a minute for the visitors center.

❹ Humboldt Lagoons State Park (p72)

Stretching out for miles along the coast, **Humboldt Lagoons** has long, sandy beaches and a string of coastal lagoons. **Big Lagoon** and prettier **Stone Lagoon** are both excellent for kayaking and bird-watching. Sunsets are spectacular, with no structures in sight. The

Stone Lagoon Visitor Center, on Hwy 101, has closed due to staffing shortages, but there's a toilet and a bulletin board displaying information. Just south of Stone Lagoon, tiny **Dry Lagoon** (a freshwater marsh) has a fantastic day hike. Park at Dry Lagoon's picnic area and hike north on the unmarked trail to Stone Lagoon; the trail skirts the southwestern shore and ends up at the ocean, passing through woods and marshland rich with wildlife. Mostly flat, it's about 2.5 miles one way – and nobody takes it because it's unmarked.

The Drive » Now, at last, you'll start to lose all perspective among the world's tallest trees. This is likely the most scenic part of the entire

Exploring Redwood National Park

trip; you'll emerge from curvy two-lane roads through redwood groves to stunning mist-shrouded shores dotted with rocky islets.

TRIP HIGHLIGHT

⑤ Redwood National Park (p72)

Heading north, **Redwood National Park** is the first park in the patchwork of state and federally administered land under the umbrella of the Redwood National & State Parks. After picking up a map at the **Kuchel Visitor Center** (☎707-465-7765; www.nps.gov/redw; Hwy 101, Orick) you'll have a suite of choices for hiking, but the half-mile stroll to **Gold Bluffs Beach** will lead you to the best spot for a picnic. Take the easy trail about another mile to **Fern Canyon**, whose 60ft, fern-covered, sheer rock walls are seen in *In the Lost World: Jurassic Park*. This is one of the most photographed spots on the North Coast – damp and lush, all emerald green – and totally worth getting your toes wet to see. Alternatively, a trip inland will get you lost in the secluded serenity of **Tall Trees Grove**. To protect the grove, a limited number of cars per day are allowed access; get permits at the visitor center. This can be a half-day trip itself, but you're well rewarded after the challenging approach (a 30-minute rumble on an old logging road, then a moderately strenuous 1.3-mile hike).

The Drive >> Follow the winding road through beautiful inland forests with views of the east and its layers of ridges and valleys, until you reach Klamath with its bear bridge. Del Norte Coast Redwoods State Park is just a few minutes up the road.

- - - - - - - - - - - -

TRIP HIGHLIGHT

6 Del Norte Coast Redwoods State Park (p73)

Marked by steep canyons and dense woods, half the 6400 acres of this **park** (vehicle day-use $8) are virgin redwood forest, crisscrossed by 15 miles of hiking trails. Even the most cynical of redwood-watchers can't help but be moved. Tall trees cling precipitously to canyon walls that drop to the rocky, timber-strewn coastline. It's almost impossible to get to the water, except via gorgeous but steep **Damnation Creek Trail** or **Footsteps Rock Trail**. The former may be only 4 miles long, but the 1100-ft elevation change and cliffside redwood makes it the park's best hike. The unmarked

---

DETOUR: NEWTON B DRURY SCENIC PARKWAY

Start: 5 Redwood National Park

Just north of Orick is the turn-off for the 8-mile parkway, which runs parallel to Hwy 101 through untouched ancient redwood forests. It's worth the short detour off the freeway to view the magnificence of these trees. Numerous trails branch off from roadside pullouts, including family- and ADA (American Disabilities Act)-friendly trails Big Tree and Revelation Trail.

---

trailhead starts from a parking area off Hwy 101 at Mile 16.

The Drive >> Leaving Del Norte Coast Redwoods State Park you'll enter dreary little Crescent City, a fine enough place to gas up or grab a bite, but not worth stopping long. North of town, Hwy 199 splits off. Take it to South Fork Rd; turn right after crossing two bridges.

- - - - - - - - - - - -

7 Jedediah Smith Redwoods State Park (p73)

The final stop on the trip is loaded with worthy superlatives – the northernmost park has the densest population of redwood and the last

natural undammed, free-flowing river in California, the sparkling Smith. All in all **Jedediah Smith Redwoods State Park** (📞707-464-6101, ext 5112; day use $8) is a jewel. The redwood here is so dense few trails penetrate the park, so instead of hiking, drive the outstanding 11-mile **Howland Hill Scenic Drive**, which cuts through otherwise inaccessible areas. It's a rough, unpaved road, and it gets graded only once a year in spring and can close if there are fallen trees or washouts, but you'll feel as if you're visiting from Lilliput.

Right Giant redwood, northern California

PATRICK ORTON / GETTY IMAGES ©

Big Sur

3

Nestled up against mossy redwood forests, the rocky Big Sur coast is a secretive place. On this overnight trip, get to know it like locals do, visiting wild beaches, waterfalls and hot springs.

TRIP HIGHLIGHTS

10 miles
Andrew Molera State Park
Where condors glide above ocean beaches

START
Bixby Bridge

3 4
5
7

14 miles
Pfeiffer Big Sur State Park
Trails to tall redwood trees

18 miles
Pfeiffer Beach
Purplish sand in a photographer's dream seascape

● Lucia
● Gorda

FINISH

Julia Pfeiffer Burns State Park
Peer out at McWay Falls

30 miles

2 DAYS
60 MILES/95KM

GREAT FOR...

BEST TIME TO GO
April to May for waterfalls and wildflowers; September to October for sunny, cloudless days.

ESSENTIAL PHOTO
McWay Falls dropping into the Pacific.

BEST FOR FAMILIES
Pfeiffer Big Sur State Park for camping, cabins and easy hikes.

Left Big Sur coastline

3 Big Sur

Much ink has been spilled extolling the raw beauty of this craggy land shoehorned between the Santa Lucia Mountains and the Pacific. Yet nothing quite prepares you for that first glimpse through the windshield of Big Sur's wild, unspoiled coastline. There are no traffic lights, banks or strip malls, and when the sun goes down, the moon and the stars are the only streetlights – if coastal fog hasn't extinguished them.

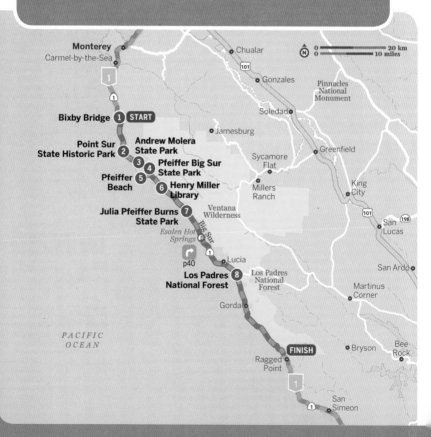

❶ Bixby Bridge

To tell the truth, Big Sur is more a state of mind than a place you can pinpoint on a map. But the photogenic **Bixby Bridge** lets you know you've finally arrived. Arching above Rainbow Canyon, this landmark is one of the world's highest single-span bridges, completed in 1932 by prisoners eager to lop time off their sentences. Stop on the north side of the bridge for an irresistible photo op.

The Drive » From Bixby Bridge, it's about 6 miles south along Hwy 1, rolling beside pasture lands, to Point Sur State Historic Park. Like everywhere else along Big Sur's coast, watch out for cyclists and use signposted roadside pullouts to let fast-moving traffic pass by.

❷ Point Sur State Historic Park

Rising like a velvety green fortress out of

LINK YOUR TRIP

1 Pacific Coast Highways

Head north on Hwy 1 for Monterey and Santa Cruz, or south to explore Santa Barbara and its famed wine country.

the sea, **Point Sur State Historic Park** (☎831-625-4419; www.pointsur.org, www.parks.ca.gov; adult/child $12/5; ☺ tours usually 1pm Wed, 10am Sat & Sun Nov-Mar, 10am & 2pm Wed & Sat, 10am Sun Apr-Oct) looks like an island, but is actually connected to the mainland by a sandbar. On the volcanic rock sits California's only turn-of-the-20th-century lightstation that's still open to the public. Ocean views and tales of the lighthouse-keepers' family lives are engrossing, especially during spooky moonlight tours. Call ahead to confirm schedules; arrive early because space is limited (no reservations).

The Drive » Lighthouse tours meet at the locked farm gate a quarter-mile north of Point Sur Naval Facility. Afterwards, drive south on Hwy 1 another 2 miles along the coast to Andrew Molera State Park.

TRIP HIGHLIGHT

❸ Andrew Molera State Park

With ocean vistas beckoning along Hwy 1, you'll be eager to put your feet on a beach by now. Named after the farmer who first planted artichokes in California, **Andrew Molera State Park** (☎831-667-2315; www.parks.ca.gov; Hwy 1; per car $10; ☺30min before sunrise-30min after sunset; 🚶) is a trail-laced pastiche of grassy meadows, ocean bluffs and sandy

beaches, all offering excellent wildlife watching. Hike for about a mile out to where the Big Sur River meets the rocky driftwood-strewn beach, whipped by strong winds and the surf. Back at the parking lot, walk south to the **Big Sur Discovery Center** (☎831-620-0702; www.ventanaws.org; admission free; ☺usually 9am-4pm Sat & Sun late May-early Sep) to learn all about endangered California condors that sometimes soar overhead.

The Drive » Speeds rarely top 35mph along Hwy 1, which narrows and becomes curvier the further south you go. Slow down a few miles beyond the state park and watch for pedestrians in 'the village,' Big Sur's hub for shops, services, motels and cafes. About 5 miles south of Andrew Molera State Park, you'll see the entrance for Pfeiffer Big Sur State Park on the inland side of the highway.

TRIP HIGHLIGHT

❹ Pfeiffer Big Sur State Park

The biggest all-natural draw on the Big Sur coast is **Pfeiffer Big Sur State Park** (☎831-667-2315; www.parks.ca.gov; 47225 Hwy 1; per car $10; ☺30min before sunrise-30min after sunset; 🚶). Named after Big Sur's first European settlers, who arrived here in 1869, it's also the largest state park along this coast. Hiking trails loop through tall redwood groves and run uphill to 60ft-high **Pfeiffer Falls**, a delicate cascade hidden in the forest that usually flows between December and May. Near the park entrance, inside a rustic lodge built in the 1930s by the Civilian Conservation Corps (CCC), you'll find a convenient general store selling cold drinks, ice cream, snacks, camping supplies and road trip souvenirs.

The Drive >> Just 2 miles south of Pfeiffer Big Sur State Park, about half a mile past ranger-staffed Big Sur Station, make a sharp right turn off Hwy 1 onto Sycamore Canyon Rd, marked only by a small yellow sign saying 'Narrow Rd.' Partly unpaved, this road (RVs and trailers prohibited) corkscrews down for over 2 miles to Pfeiffer Beach.

- - - - - - - - - -

TRIP HIGHLIGHT

⑤ Pfeiffer Beach

Hidden down a side road to the sea, **Pfeiffer Beach** (☎831-667-2315; www.fs.fed.us/r5/lospadres; Sycamore Canyon Rd; per

car $10; ☉9am-8pm; 🅿️👶) is worth the trouble it takes to reach it. This phenomenal, crescent-shaped strand is known for its huge double rock formation, through which waves crash with life-affirming power. It's often windy, and the surf is too dangerous for swimming. But dig down into the wet sand – it's purple! That's because manganese garnet washes down from the craggy hillsides above.

The Drive >> Backtrack up narrow, winding Sycamore Canyon Rd for more than 2 miles, then turn right onto Hwy 1 southbound. After two more twisting, slow-moving miles, look for Nepenthe restaurant on your right. The Henry Miller Library is another 0.4 miles south, at a hairpin turn on your left.

- - - - - - - - - -

⑥ Henry Miller Library

'It was here in Big Sur I first learned to say Amen!' wrote Henry Miller, a surrealist novelist and local resident from 1944 to 1962. More of a beatnik memorial, alt-cultural venue and bookshop, the **Henry Miller Library** (☎831-667-2574; www.henrymiller.org; 48603 Hwy 1; admission by donation; ☉11am-6pm; @🛜) was never actually the writer's home. The house belonged to Miller's friend, painter Emil White. Inside are copies of all of Miller's published books, many of his paintings and a collection of Big Sur and Beat Generation material. Stop by to browse and hang out on the front deck with coffee, or join the bohemian carnival of live music, open-mic nights and independent film screenings.

The Drive >> You'll leave most of the traffic behind as Hwy 1 continues southbound, curving slowly along the vertiginous cliffs, occasionally opening up for ocean panoramas. It's fewer than 8 miles to Julia Pfeiffer

**DETOUR:
ESALEN HOT SPRINGS**

Start: ⑦ Julia Pfeiffer Burns State Park

Ocean beaches and waterfalls aren't the only places to get wet in Big Sur. At private **Esalen Institute** (☎831-667-3047; 55000 Hwy 1; hot-springs entry $25, credit cards only; ☉public access 1am-3am, by reservation only), clothing-optional baths fed by a natural hot spring sit on a ledge above the ocean. Dollars to donuts you'll never take another dip that compares scenery-wise, especially on stormy winter nights. Only two small outdoor pools perch directly over the waves, so once you've stripped and taken a quick shower, head outside immediately. Advance telephone reservations are required. The signposted entrance is on Hwy 1, about 3 miles south of Julia Pfeiffer Burns State Park.

AMIT BASU PHOTOGRAPHY / GETTY IMAGES ©

Julia Pfeiffer Burns State Park

Burns State Park; the entrance is on the inland side of Hwy 1.

TRIP HIGHLIGHT

❼ Julia Pfeiffer Burns State Park

If you've got an appetite for chasing waterfalls, swing into **Julia Pfeiffer Burns State Park** (☏831-667-2315; www.parks.ca.gov; Hwy 1; per car $10; ⏱30min before sunrise-30min after sunset; 🚻). From the parking lot, the short Overlook Trail rushes downhill towards the sea, passing through a tunnel underneath Hwy 1. Everyone is in a hurry to see **McWay Falls**, which tumbles year-round over granite cliffs and free-falls into the ocean – or the beach, depending on the tide. This is the classic Big Sur postcard shot, with tree-topped rocks jutting above a golden beach next to swirling blue pools and crashing white surf. During winter, watch for migrating whales offshore.

The Drive » The tortuously winding stretch of Hwy 1 southbound is sparsely populated, rugged and remote, running through national forest. Make sure you've got enough fuel in the tank to at least reach the expensive gas station at Gorda, over 20 miles south of Julia Pfeiffer Burns State Park.

❽ Los Padres National Forest

About 5 miles south of Nacimiento-Fergusson Rd, **Sand Dollar Beach Picnic Area** (www.fs.usda.gov; per vehicle $10; ⏱9am-8pm) faces southern Big Sur's longest sandy beach, protected by high bluffs.

Once you pass Plaskett Creek Campground, look for trails down to **Jade Cove** from roadside pull-offs along Hwy 1. In 1971, local divers recovered a 9000lb jade boulder here that measured 8ft long and was valued at $180,000!

If you have any slivers of sunlight left, keep trucking down Hwy 1 approximately 8 miles past Gorda to **Salmon Creek Falls** (www.fs.fed.us/r5/lospadres; Hwy 1; admission free; 🚻🐾), which usually runs from December through May. Take a short hike to splash around in the pools at the base of this double-drop waterfall, tucked uphill in a forested canyon. In a hairpin turn of Hwy 1, the roadside turnoff is marked only by a small brown trailhead sign.

Disneyland & Orange County Beaches

4

Let the kids loose at the 'Happiest Place on Earth,' then strike out for sunny SoCal beaches – as seen on TV and the silver screen. It's impossible not to have fun on this coastal getaway.

TRIP HIGHLIGHTS

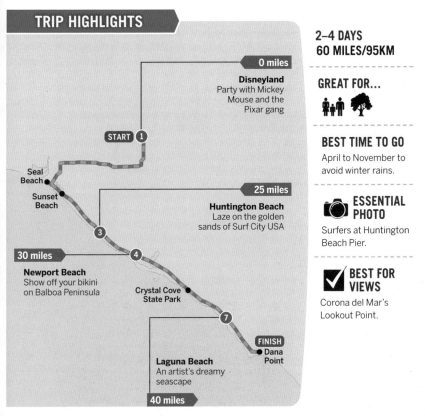

0 miles

Disneyland
Party with Mickey Mouse and the Pixar gang

START ①

Seal Beach

Sunset Beach

25 miles

Huntington Beach
Laze on the golden sands of Surf City USA

③

④

30 miles

Newport Beach
Show off your bikini on Balboa Peninsula

Crystal Cove State Park

⑦

FINISH
Dana Point

Laguna Beach
An artist's dreamy seascape

40 miles

**2–4 DAYS
60 MILES/95KM**

GREAT FOR...

BEST TIME TO GO
April to November to avoid winter rains.

ESSENTIAL PHOTO
Surfers at Huntington Beach Pier.

BEST FOR VIEWS
Corona del Mar's Lookout Point.

Left Surfers on Huntington Beach

4

Disneyland & Orange County Beaches

It's true you'll find gorgeous sunsets, prime surfing breaks and just-off-the-boat seafood when road tripping down the OC's sun-kissed coastal Hwy 1. Yet it's the unexpected and serendipitous discoveries you'll remember long after you've left this blissful 42 miles of surf and sand behind. Top it all off with a day or two at Disneyland's theme parks, and let's call it a wrap for the perfect SoCal family vacation.

1 Disneyland (p98)

No SoCal theme park welcomes more millions of visitors every year than **Disneyland** (☎714-781-4636; www.disneyland.com; 1313 S Harbor Blvd; 1-day single-park admission adult/child $96/90, 2-park day pass $135/129; ⊞). From the ghostly skeletons of Pirates of the Caribbean to the screeching monkeys of the Indiana Jones Adventure, there's magical detail everywhere. Retro-futuristic Tomorrowland is where the Finding Nemo Submarine Voyage and *Star Wars*–themed Star Tours and Jedi Training Academy await. Use the Fastpass system and you'll be hurtling through Space Mountain – still the park's best adrenaline pumper – in no time. After dark, watch

LINK YOUR TRIP

1 Pacific Coast Highways

Orange County is California's official section of the Pacific Coast Hwy (PCH), running along Hwy 1 between laidback Seal Beach and Dana Point.

fireworks explode over Sleeping Beauty's Castle.

Any fear of heights? Then ditch the Twilight Zone Tower of Terror at **Disney's California Adventure** (DCA), Disneyland's newer neighbor. DCA's lightheartedly themed areas highlight the best of the Golden State, while plenty of adventures like Route 66–themed Cars Land don't involve losing your lunch. An exception is rockin' California Screamin' at Paradise Pier: this whip-fast coaster looks like an old-school carnival ride, but from the moment it blasts forward with a cannon-shot whoosh, this monster never lets go. Catch the enthusiasm of the Pixar Play Parade by day and World of Color special-effects show at night.

Just outside the parks, **Downtown Disney** pedestrian mall is packed with souvenir shops, family restaurants, after-dark bars and entertainment venues and, in summer, live musicians playing for the crowds.

The Drive » Follow Harbor Blvd south for 3 not-very-scenic miles, then take Hwy 22 west through inland Orange County, merging onto the I-405 north. After another mile or so, exit onto Seal Beach Blvd, which crawls 3 miles toward the coast. Turn right onto Hwy 1, also known as the Pacific Coast Hwy (PCH) throughout Orange

County, then take a left onto Main St in Seal Beach.

2 Seal Beach

In the SoCal beauty pageant for pint-sized beach towns, Seal Beach is the winner of the crown. Stop here and you'll discover it's a refreshingly unhurried alternative to the more crowded Orange County coast further south. Its three-block **Main St** is a stoplight-free zone that bustles with mom-and-pop restaurants and indie shops that are low on 'tude and high on nostalgia. Follow the path of barefoot surfers as they trot toward the beach to where Main St ends, then walk out onto **Seal Beach Pier**. The 1906 original first fell victim to winter storms in the 1930s, and since then it has been rebuilt three times with a splintery, wooden boardwalk. Down on the **beach**, you'll find families spread out on blankets, building sandcastles and playing in the water – all of them ignoring that hideous oil derrick offshore. The gentle waves make Seal Beach a great place to learn to surf. **M&M Surfing School** (☎714-846-7873; www.surfingschool.com; group lesson from $72, wetsuit/surfboard rental $15/25; ⊞) parks their van in the lot just north of

HUNTINGTON CITY BEACH

LOCAL KNOWLEDGE
VERONICA HILL

'California Travel Tips' YouTube host

Want to get the most bang for your buck at Disneyland or Disney's California Adventure? If your kids are too young to ride, ask for the rider-switch pass. Grab it from a cast member as you enter the ride (while your partner watches the kids). Afterward, give the pass to your partner so they can whisk through the FASTPASS line. If you have an impatient teenager, send them through the single-rider line instead.

Top: Huntington Beach
Left & right: Beach time, southern California

MATTHEW MICAH WRIGHT / GETTY IMAGES ©

the pier, off Ocean Ave at 8th St.

The Drive » Past a short bridge farther south along Hwy 1, drivers drop onto a mile-long spit of land known as Sunset Beach, with its biker bars and harborside kayak and stand-up paddle boarding (SUP) rental shops. Keep cruising Hwy 1 south another 6 miles past Bolsa Chica State Beach and Ecological Reserve to Huntington Beach Pier.

TRIP HIGHLIGHT

3 Huntington Beach (p104)

In 'Surf City USA,' SoCal obsession's with wave riding hits its frenzied peak. There's a statue of Hawaiian surfer Duke Kahanamoku at the intersection of Main St and PCH, and if you look down, you'll see names of legendary surfers in the sidewalk **Surfers' Hall of Fame** (www.hsssurf.com/shof/). A few blocks east, the **International Surfing Museum** (714-960-3483; www.surfingmuseum.org; 411 Olive Ave; suggested donation $2; noon-5pm Mon-Fri, 11am-6pm Sat & Sun) honors those same legends. Then join the crowds on the **Huntington Beach Pier**, where you can catch up-close views of daredevils barreling through tubes. The surf here may not be the ideal place to test your newbie skills, however – locals can be territorial. In summer, the US Open of Surfing draws more than 600 world-class surfers and 400,000 spectators with a minivillage of concerts, motocross demos and skater jams. As for **Huntington City Beach** itself, it's wide and flat – a perfect place to snooze on the sand on a giant beach towel. Snag a fire pit just south of the pier to build an evening bonfire with friends.

The Drive >> From the Huntington Beach Pier at the intersection of Main St, drive south on Hwy 1 (PCH) alongside the ocean for another 4 miles to Newport Beach. Turn right onto W Balboa Blvd, leading onto the Balboa Peninsula, squeezed between the ocean and Balboa Island, off Newport Harbor.

TRIP HIGHLIGHT

④ Newport Beach (p103)

As seen on Bravo's *Real Housewives of Orange County* and Fox's

The OC and *Arrested Development,* in glitzy Newport Beach wealthy socialites, glamorous teens and gorgeous beaches all share the spotlight. Bikini vixens strut down the sandy beach stretching between the peninsula's twin piers, while boogie boarders brave human-eating waves at the **Wedge** and the ballet of yachts in the harbor makes you dream of being rich and famous. From the harbor, hop aboard a ferry over to old-fashioned **Balboa Island** or climb aboard the carousel by the landmark 1905 **Balboa Pavilion**. The Ferris wheel still spins at pint-sized **Balboa Fun Zone** (www.thebalboafunzone. com; per ride $4; ⊙11am-8pm Sun-Thu, to 9pm Fri, to 10pm Sat; ♿), nearby the **Newport Harbor Nautical Museum** (☎949-675-8915;

http://explorocean.org; 600 E Bay Ave; adult/child $5/3; ⊙noon-4pm Wed & Thu, to 5pm Fri-Sun; ♿). Just inland, visit the cutting-edge contemporary **Orange County Museum of Art** (☎949-759-1122; www.ocma.net; 850 San Clemente Dr; adult/child $12/ free; ⊙11am-5pm Wed-Sun, to 8pm Thu) to escape SoCal's vainglorious pop culture.

The Drive >> South of Newport Beach, prime-time ocean views are just a short detour off Hwy 1. First drive south across the bridge over Newport Channel, then after 3 miles turn right onto Marguerite Ave in Corona del Mar. Once you reach the coast, take another right onto Ocean Blvd.

---

⑤ Corona del Mar

Savor some of SoCal's most celebrated ocean views from the bluffs of Corona del Mar, a chichi bedroom community south of Newport

---

↱ DETOUR: KNOTT'S BERRY FARM

Start: ❶ Disneyland

Hear the screams? Got teens? Hello, **Knott's Berry Farm** (☎714-220-5200; www. knotts.com; 8039 Beach Blvd, Buena Park; adult/child $62/33; ⊙open daily from 10am, closing times vary; ♿), America's first theme park, which opened in 1940. Today high-scream coasters lure fast-track fanatics. Look up as you enter to see the bare feet of riders who've removed their flip-flops for the Silver Bullet, the suspended coaster careening past overhead, famed for its corkscrew, double spiral and outside loop. In October, Knott's hosts SoCal's scariest after-dark Halloween party. Year-round, the *Peanuts* gang keeps moppets happy in Camp Snoopy, while the next-door water park **Knott's Soak City USA** (☎714-220-5200; www.soakcityoc.com; adult/child $27/22; ⊙open mid-May–Sep, hr vary; ♿) keeps you cool on blazing-hot summer days. Knott's is a 20-minute drive from Disneyland via I-5 north to La Palma Ave west.

Channel. Several postcard beaches, rocky coves and child-friendly tidepools beckon along this idyllic stretch of coast. One of the best viewpoints is at breezy **Lookout Point** on Ocean Blvd near Heliotrope Ave. Below the rocky cliffs to the east is half-mile long Main Beach, officially **Corona del Mar State Beach** (☎949-644-3151; www.parks.ca.gov; entry per vehicle $15; ☷6am-10pm), with fire rings and volleyball courts (arrive early on weekends to get a parking spot). Stairs lead down to Pirates Cove which has a great, waveless pocket beach for families – scenes from *Gilligan's Island* were shot here. Head east on Ocean Blvd to **Inspiration Point**, near the corner of Orchid Ave, for more vistas of surf, sand and sea.

The Drive ›› Follow Orchid Ave back north to Hwy 1, then turn right and drive southbound. Traffic thins out as ocean views become more wild and uncluttered by housing developments that head up into the hills on your left. It's just a couple of miles to the entrance of Crystal Cove State Park.

- - - - - - - - - - - - - -

❻ Crystal Cove State Park

With 3.5 miles of open beach and over 2300 acres of undeveloped woodland, **Crystal Cove State Park** (☎949-494-3539; www.parks.ca.gov, www.crystalcovestatepark.com; entry per vehicle $15; ☷6am-sunset) lets you almost forget that you're in a crowded metro area. That is, once you get past the parking lot and stake out a place on the sand. Many visitors don't know it, but it's also an underwater park where scuba enthusiasts can check out the wreck of a Navy Corsair fighter plane that went down in 1949. Or just go tidepooling, fishing, kayaking and surfing along Crystal Cove's exhilaratingly wild, windy shoreline. On the inland side of Hwy 1, miles of hiking and mountain biking trails wait for landlubbers.

The Drive ›› Drive south on Hwy 1 for another 4 miles or so. As shops, restaurants, art galleries, motels and hotels start to crowd the highway once again, you've arrived in Laguna

49

DETOUR: PACIFIC MARINE MAMMAL CENTER

Start: 7 Laguna Beach

About 3 miles northeast of Laguna Beach is the heart-warming **Pacific Marine Mammal Center** (☎949-494-3050; www.pacificmmc.org; 20612 Laguna Canyon Rd; admission by donation; ☺10am-4pm; ♿), dedicated to rescuing and rehabilitating injured or ill marine mammals. This nonprofit center has a small staff and many volunteers who help nurse rescued pinnipeds (mostly sea lions and seals) back to health before releasing them into the wild. Stop by and take a self-guided facility tour to learn more about these marine mammals and to visit the 'patients' out back.

Beach. Downtown is a maze of one-way streets just east of the Laguna Canyon Rd (Hwy 133) intersection.

TRIP HIGHLIGHT

7 Laguna Beach (p102)

This early 20th-century artist colony's secluded coves, romantic-looking cliffs and Arts and Crafts bungalows come as a relief after miles of suburban beige-box architecture. With joie de vivre, Laguna celebrates its bohemian roots with summer arts festivals, dozens of galleries and the acclaimed **Laguna Art Museum** (☎949-494-8971; www.lagunaartmuseum.org; 307 Cliff Dr; adult/child $7/free; ☺11am-5pm Fri-Tue, to 9pm Thu). In downtown's village, it's

easy to while away an afternoon browsing the chic boutiques. Down on the shore, **Main Beach** is crowded with volleyball players and sunbathers. Just north atop the bluffs, **Heisler Park** winds past public art, palm trees, picnic tables and grand views of rocky shores and tidepools. Drop down to Divers Cove, a deep, protected inlet. Heading south, dozens of public beaches sprawl along just a few miles of coastline. Keep a sharp eye out for 'beach access' signs off Hwy 1, or pull into locals' favorite **Aliso Beach County Park** (www.ocparks.com/alisobeach; 31131 S Pacific Coast Hwy; parking per hr $1; ☺6am-10pm).

The Drive » Keep driving south of downtown Laguna

Beach on Hwy 1 (PCH) for about 3 miles to Aliso Beach County Park, then another 4 miles into the town of Dana Point. Turn right onto Green Lantern St, then left onto Cove Rd, which winds past the state beach and Ocean Institute onto Dana Point Harbor Dr.

---

8 Dana Point

Last up is marina-flanked Dana Point, the namesake of 19th-century adventurer Richard Dana, who famously called the area 'the only romantic spot on the coast.' These days it's more about family fun and sportfishing boats at **Dana Point Harbor**. Designed for kids, the **Ocean Institute** (☎949-496-2274; www.ocean-institute.org; 24200 Dana Pt Harbor Dr; adult/child $6.50/4.50; ☺10am-3pm Sat & Sun; ♿) owns replicas of historic tall ships, maritime-related exhibits and a floating research lab. East of the harbor, **Doheny State Beach** (☎949-496-6172; www.parks.ca.gov, www.dohenystatebeach.org; entry per vehicle $15; ☺6am-10pm, to 8pm Nov-Feb; ♿) is where you'll find picnic tables, volleyball courts, an oceanfront bike path and a sandy beach for swimming, surfing, tidepooling and scuba diving.

Destinations

San Francisco (p54)
Get to know the capital of weird from the inside out.

Northern Coast & Redwoods (p66)
View redwood forests along NorCal's wild coastline.

Central Coast (p74)
Surf Santa Cruz' coast and whale-watch at Monterey.

Santa Barbara County (p82)
Explore vineyards just outside Santa Barbara town.

Los Angeles (p90)
Discover La La Land beyond her beaches and celebs.

Disneyland & Orange County (p98)
Head to Disney's Magic Kingdom or hit SoCal's beaches.

San Diego (p106)
Wander the world-famous zoo and first-class museums.

View across Telegraph Hill and Coit Tower, San Francisco

San Francisco

San Francisco's morning fog erases the boundaries between land and ocean, reality and infinite possibility.

👁 Sights

Golden Gate Bridge
Bridge

(www.goldengatebridge.org/visitors; off Lincoln Blvd; northbound free, southbound toll $6, billed electronically to vehicle's license plate; 🚌28, all Golden Gate Transit buses) Hard to believe the Navy almost nixed SF's signature art-deco landmark by architects Gertrude and Irving Murrow and engineer Joseph B Strauss. Photographers, take your cue from Hitchcock: seen from Fort Point (🗲415-556-1693; www.nps.gov/fopo; Marine Dr; admission free; ⊙10am-5pm Fri-Sun; 🅿; 🚌28) FREE, the 1937 bridge induces a thrilling case of vertigo. Fog aficionados prefer Marin's Vista Point, watching gusts billow through bridge cables like dry ice at a Kiss concert. For the full effect, hike or bike the 2-mile span.

Alcatraz
Historic Site

See p56.

Coit Tower
Tower

(🗲415-362-0808; http://sfrecpark.org/destination/telegraph-hill-pioneer-park/coit-tower; Telegraph Hill Blvd; elevator entry (nonresident) adult/child $7/5; ⊙10am-5:30pm Mar-Sep, 9am-4:30pm Oct-Feb; 🚌39) Adding an exclamation mark to San Francisco's landscape, Coit Tower offers views worth shouting about – especially after you climb the giddy, steep Filbert St or Greenwich St steps to the top of Telegraph Hill. This

210ft, peculiar projectile is a monument to San Francisco firefighters financed by eccentric heiress Lillie Hitchcock Coit. Lillie could drink, smoke and play cards as well as any off-duty firefighter, rarely missed a fire or a fire-fighter's funeral, and even had the firehouse emblem embroidered on her bedsheets.

Asian Art Museum
Museum

(🗲415-581-3500; www.asianart.org; 200 Larkin St; adult/student/child $12/8/free, 1st Sun of month free; ⊙10am-5pm Tue-Sun, to 9pm Thu; 🚹; Ⓜ Civic Center, Ⓑ Civic Center) Imaginations race from ancient Persian miniatures to cutting-edge Japanese architecture through three floors spanning 6000 years of Asian arts. Besides the largest Asian art collection outside Asia – 18,000 works – the Asian offers excellent programs for all ages, from shadow-puppet shows and yoga for kids to weeknight Artist's Drawing Club mixers with crosscultural DJ mashups.

City Lights Bookstore
Building

(🗲415-362-8193; www.citylights.com; 261 Columbus Ave; ⊙10am-midnight) When founder and Beat poet Lawrence Ferlinghetti and manager Shigeyoshi Murao defended their right to 'willfully and lewdly print' Allen Ginsberg's magnificent *Howl and Other Poems* in 1957, City Lights became a free-speech landmark. Celebrate your freedom to read freely in the designated Poet's Chair upstairs overlooking Jack Kerouac Alley, load up on 'zines on the mezzanine and entertain radical ideas downstairs in the Muckracking and Stolen Continents sections.

Exploratorium
Museum

(☑ 415-528-4444; www.exploratorium.edu; Pier 15; adult/child $25/19, Thu evening $15; ⊙10am-5pm Tue-Sun, over-18yr only Thu 6-10pm; P ♿; M F) ✐ Is there a science to skateboarding? Do toilets flush conterclockwise in Australia? Find out first-hand with 600-plus fascinating, freaky exhibits. In under an hour you can star in psychedelic fractal music videos, make art from bacteria, and grope your way in total darkness through the Tactile Dome. Founded in 1969 by atom-bomb physicist Frank Oppenheimer, the newly relocated, expanded Exploratorium shows how life is cooler than science fiction.

Musée Mécanique
Amusement Park

(☑ 415-346-2000; www.museemechanique.org; Pier 45, Shed A; ⊙10am-7pm Mon-Fri, to 8pm Sat & Sun; ♿; ☐47, ☐ Powell-Mason, Powell-Hyde, M F) Where else can you guillotine a man for a quarter? Creepy, 19th-century arcade games like the macabre French Execution compete for your spare change with the diabolical Ms Pac-Man.

Crissy Field
Park

(www.crissyfield.org; 1199 East Beach; ☐30, PresidioGo Shuttle) The Presidio's army airstrip has been stripped of asphalt and reinvented as a haven for coastal birds, kite-fliers and windsurfers enjoying sweeping views of Golden Gate Bridge.

Baker Beach
Beach

(⊙sunrise-sunset; ☐29, PresidioGo Shuttle) Un-swimmable waters (except when the tide's coming in) but unbeatable views of the Golden Gate make this former Army beachhead SF's tanning location of choice, especially the clothing-optional north end – at least until the afternoon fog rolls in.

826 Valencia
Cultural Site

(☑ 415-642-5905; www.826valencia.org; 826 Valencia St; ⊙noon-6pm; ♿; ☐14, 33, 49, ☐16th St Mission, M J) Avast, ye scurvy scalawags! If ye be shipwrecked without yer eye patch or Mc-Sweeney's literary anthology, lay down yer dubloons and claim yer booty at this here nonprofit Pirate Store. Below decks, kids be writing tall tales for dark nights asea, and ye can study making video games and maga-

NEIGHBORHOODS IN A NUTSHELL

North Beach & the Hills Poetry and parrots, top-of-the-world views, Italian gossip and opera on the jukebox.

Embarcadero & the Piers Weird science, sea-lion antics, gourmet treats, and getaways to and from Alcatraz.

Downtown & the Financial District The notorious Barbary Coast has gone legit with banks and boutiques, but shows its wild side in redwood parks and provocative art.

Chinatown Pagoda roofs, mahjong games, revolutionary plots, and fortunes made and lost in historic alleyways.

Hayes Valley, Civic Center & the Tenderloin Grand buildings and great performances, dive bars and cable cars, foodie finds and local designs.

SoMa South of Market; where high technology meets higher art, and everyone gets down and dirty on the dance floor.

Mission A book in one hand, a burrito in the other, and murals all around.

Castro Out and proud with rainbow sidewalks and history-making policy platforms.

Haight Flashbacks and fashion-forwardness, free thinking, free music and pricey skateboards.

Japantown, the Fillmore & Pacific Heights Sushi in the fountains, John Coltrane over the altar, and rock at the Fillmore.

Marina & the Presidio Boutiques, organic dining, peace and public nudity at a former army base.

Golden Gate Park & the Avenues SF's great green streak, surrounded by gourmet hangouts for hungry surfers.

Alcatraz

Book a ferry from Pier 33 and ride 1.5 miles across the bay to explore America's most notorious former prison. The trip itself is worth the money, providing stunning views of the city skyline. Once you've landed at the **Ferry Dock & Pier 1**, you begin the 580-yard walk to the top of the island and prison; if you're out of shape, there's a twice-hourly tram.

As you climb toward the **Guardhouse 2**, notice the island's steep slope; before it was a prison, Alcatraz was a fort. In the 1850s, the military quarried the rocky shores into near-vertical cliffs. Ships could then only dock at a single port, separated from the main buildings by a sally port (a drawbridge and moat in what became the guardhouse). Inside, peer through floor grates to see Alcatraz' original prison.

Volunteers tend the brilliant **Officer's Row Gardens 3** – an orderly counterpoint to the overgrown rose bushes surrounding the burned-out shell of the **Warden's House 4**. At the top of the hill, by the front door of the **Main Cellhouse 5**, beauty shots unfurl all around, including a **view of the Golden Gate Bridge 6**. Above the main door of the administration building, notice the **historic signs & graffiti 7**, before you step inside the dank, cold prison to find the **Frank Morris cell 8**, former home to Alcatraz' most notorious jail-breaker.

TOP TIPS

➜ Book at least two weeks prior for self-guided daytime visits, longer for ranger-led night tours. For info on garden tours, see www.alcatraz gardens.org.

➜ Be prepared to hike; a steep path ascends from the ferry landing to the cell block. Most people spend two to three hours on the island. You need only reserve for the outbound ferry; take any ferry back.

➜ There's no food (just water) but you can bring your own; picnicking is allowed at the ferry dock only. Dress in layers as weather changes fast and it's usually windy.

JOHN A VLAHIDES ©

Historic Signs & Graffiti
During their 1969–71 occupation, Native Americans graffitied the water tower: 'Home of the Free Indian Land.' Above the cellhouse door, examine the eagle-and-flag crest to see how the red-and-white stripes were changed to spell 'Free.'

Warden's House
Fires destroyed the warden's house and other structures during the Indian Occupation. The government blamed the Native Americans; the Native Americans blamed agents provocateurs acting on behalf of the Nixon Administration to undermine public sympathy.

Parade Grounds

DAVID CLAPP / GETTY IMAGES ©

Ferry Dock & Pier
A giant wall map helps you get your bearings. Inside nearby Bldg 64, short films and exhibits provide historical perspective on the prison and details about the Indian Occupation.

View of Golden Gate Bridge
The Golden Gate Bridge stretches wide on the horizon. Best views are from atop the island at Eagle Plaza, near the cellhouse entrance, and at water level along the Agave Trail (September to January only).

Main Cellhouse
During the mid-20th century, the maximum-security prison housed the day's most notorious troublemakers, including Al Capone and Robert Stroud, the 'Birdman of Alcatraz' (who actually conducted his ornithology studies at Leavenworth).

Power House

Recreation Yard

Water Tower

6

Officers' Club

5

8

Frank Morris Cell
Peer into cell 138 on B-Block to see a re-creation of the dummy's head that Frank Morris left in his bed as a decoy to aid his notorious – and successful – 1962 escape from Alcatraz.

7

Lighthouse

3

4

2

Guard Tower

1

Guardhouse
Alcatraz' oldest building dates to 1857 and retains remnants of the original drawbridge and moat. During the Civil War the basement was transformed into a military dungeon – the genesis of Alcatraz as prison.

Officer's Row Gardens
In the 19th century soldiers imported topsoil to beautify the island with gardens. Well-trusted prisoners later gardened – Elliott Michener said it kept him sane. Historians, ornithologists and archaeologists choose today's plants.

Downtown San Francisco & SoMa

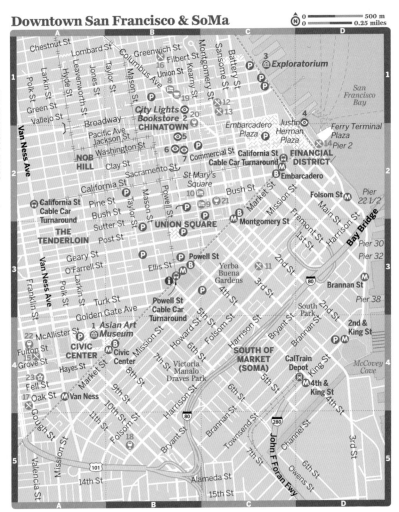

zines and suchlike, if that be yer dastardly inclination...arrrr!

☞ Tours

Day visits to Alcatraz (www.nps.gov/alca) include captivating audio tours with prisoners and guards recalling cellhouse life, while creepy twilight tours are led by park rangers; book tickets at least two weeks ahead. See also p56.

Alcatraz Cruises   Boat Tour

(☎415-981-7625; www.alcatrazcruises.com; day tours adult/child/family $30/18/92, night adult/child $37/22) Ferries depart Pier 33 half-hourly 9am to 3:55pm, night tours leave at 6:10pm and 6:45pm.

Precita Eyes Mission Mural Tours   Tour

(☎415-285-2287; www.precitaeyes.org; adult $15-20, child $3; ⊙ see website calendar for tour dates; 👫) Muralists lead two-hour tours on foot or bike covering 60 to 70 murals in a six- to 10-block radius of mural-bedecked Balmy Alley; proceeds fund mural upkeep at this community arts nonprofit.

Downtown San Francisco & SoMa

Chinatown Alleyway Tours Tour

(☑415-984-1478; www.chinatownalleywaytours. org; adult/student $18/12; ☺11am Sat; ♿; 🚌8X, 8AX, 8BX) Neighborhood teens lead two-hour community nonprofit tours for up-close-and-personal peeks into Chinatown's past (weather permitting). Book five days ahead or pay double for Saturday walk-ins; cash only.

✨ Festivals & Events

February

Lunar New Year Cultural

(www.chineseparade.com) Firecrackers, legions of tiny-tot martial artists and a 200ft dancing dragon make this parade the highlight of San Francisco winters.

April & May

SF International Film Festival Film

(www.sffs.org) Stars align and directors launch premieres each April at the nation's oldest film festival.

Bay to Breakers Sport

(www.baytobreakers.com; race registration $58-89.50) Run costumed from Embarcadero to Ocean Beach (7.5 miles) on the third Sunday in May.

June

SF Pride Celebration Cultural

A day isn't enough to do SF proud: June begins with International LGBT Film Festival

(www.frameline.org; ☺mid-Jun) and goes out in style the last weekend with Pink Saturday's Dyke March (www.dykemarch.org) and Pride Parade (www.sfpride.org).

August & September

Outside Lands Music

(www.sfoutsidelands.com/; 1-/3-day $115/375) Three days of major acts – such as Kanye West, Macklemore, The Killers, The Flaming Lips – and outlandish debauchery at Wine Land, Beer Lands and Taste of the Bay.

Folsom Street Fair Street Fair

(www.folsomstreetfair.com) Work that leather look and enjoy public spankings for local charities the last weekend of September.

October & November

Litquake Literature

(www.litquake.org) Score signed books and grab drinks with authors in October.

Hardly Strictly Bluegrass Music

(www.strictlybluegrass.com) Three days of free Golden Gate Park concerts and headliners ranging from Elvis Costello to Gillian Welch; early October.

Día de los Muertos Festival

(Day of the Dead; www.dayofthedeadsf.org) Party to wake the dead with a spooky costume parade, sugar skulls and fabulous altars in the Mission on November 2.

Sleeping

Hotel des Arts
Hotel $

(☑415-956-3232, 800-956-4322; www.sfhoteldesarts.com; 447 Bush St; r with bath $129-199, without bath $99; 🛜; Ⓜ Montgomery, Ⓑ Montgomery) A budget hotel for art freaks, with jaw-dropping murals by underground artists – it's like sleeping inside a painting. Rooms with private bath require seven-night stays. Bring earplugs.

HI San Francisco
Fisherman's Wharf
Hostel $

(☑415-771-7277; www.sfhostels.com; Bldg 240, Fort Mason; dm incl breakfast $30-42, r $75-109; Ⓟ @ 🛜; 🚌28, 30, 47, 49) A former army hospital building offers bargain-priced private rooms and dorms (some co-ed) with four to 22 beds and a huge kitchen. No curfew, but no heat during the day – bring warm clothes. Limited free parking.

Inn San Francisco
B&B $$

(☑800-359-0913, 415-641-0188; www.innsf.com; 943 S Van Ness Ave; r incl breakfast $185-310, with shared bath $135-200; Ⓟ @ 🛜; 🚌14, 49) 🍃 An impeccably maintained 1872 Italianate-Victorian mansion, this inn has period antiques, fresh-cut flowers, and fluffy featherbeds; some have Jacuzzi tubs. There's also a freestanding garden cottage that sleeps up to six. Outside there's an English garden and redwood hot tub. Limited parking: reserve ahead.

★ DON'T MISS:
GOLDEN GATE PARK

When San Franciscans refer to 'the park,' there's only one that gets the definite article. Everything they hold dear is in Golden Gate Park (http://sfrecpark.org; 👫 🐾; 🚌5, 18, 21, 28, 29, 33, 44, 71, Ⓜ N) 🍃, including free spirits, free music, Frisbee and bison.

The park offers 7.5 miles of bicycle trails, 12 miles of equestrian trails, an archery range, fly-casting pools, four soccer fields and 21 tennis courts. Sundays, when JFK Dr closes to traffic around 9th Ave, don't miss roller disco and lindy-hopping in the park. Other times, catch these park highlights:

MH de Young Museum (☑415-750-3600; http://deyoung.famsf.org/; 50 Hagiwara Tea Garden Dr; adult/child $10/6, discount with Muni ticket $2, 1st Tue of month free, online booking fee $1 per ticket; ⊙9:30am-5:15pm Tue-Sun, to 8:45pm Fri Apr-Nov; 🚌5, 44, 71, Ⓜ N) Follow sculptor Andy Goldsworthy's artificial earthquake fault in the sidewalk into Herzog + de Meuron's faultlessly sleek, copper-clad building that's oxidizing green to blend into the park. Don't be fooled by the de Young's camouflaged exterior: shows here boldly broaden artistic horizons, from Oceanic ceremonial masks and Bulgari jewels to California photographer Anthony Friedkin's 1970s portraits of gay liberation.

California Academy of Sciences (☑415-379-8000; www.calacademy.org; 55 Music Concourse Dr; adult/child $34.95/24.95, discount with Muni ticket $3; ⊙9:30am-5pm Mon-Sat, 11am-5pm Sun; Ⓟ 👫; 🚌5, 6, 31, 33, 44, 71, Ⓜ N) Architect Renzo Piano's landmark, LEED-certified green building houses 38,000 weird and wonderful animals, with a four-story rainforest and split-level aquarium under a 'living roof' of California wildflowers. After the penguins nod off to sleep, the wild rumpus starts at kids'-only Academy Sleepovers and over-21 NightLife Thursdays, when rainforest-themed cocktails encourage strange mating rituals among shy first dates.

Japanese Tea Garden (☑tea ceremony reservations 415-752-1171; www.japaneseteagardensf.com; 75 Hagiwara Tea Garden Dr; adult/child $7/2, before 10am Mon, Wed & Fri free; ⊙9am-6pm Mar-Oct, to 4:45pm Nov-Feb; Ⓟ 👫; 🚌5, 44, 71, Ⓜ N) Since 1894, this 5-acre garden has blushed with cherry blossoms in spring, turned flaming red with maple leaves in fall, and lost all track of time in the meditative Zen Garden. The 100-year-old bonsai grove is the legacy of founder Makoto Hagiwara, who tended them until his family's forced deportation to WWII Japanese American internment camps, and spent decades afterwards restoring these priceless miniature evergreens. Don't miss green tea and fortune cookies (invented for the garden's opening) at the tea pavilion.

Orchard Garden Hotel
Boutique Hotel $$$

(☑415-399-9807, 888-717-2881; www.theorchard
gardenhotel.com; 466 Bush St; r $295-370;
✱◉☜; ❑2, 3, 30, 45, ⒷMontgomery) ⫸ San
Francisco's first all-green-practices hotel
features sustainable wood furnishings,
chemical-free cleaning products, and a
sunny rooftop terrace. Luxe touches in-
clude fluffy down pillows and Egyptian-
cotton sheets in soothingly quiet rooms.

San Remo Hotel
Hotel $$

(☑415-776-8688, 800-352-7366; www.sanremohotel.
com; 2237 Mason St; r with shared bath $99-139;
◉☜☀; ❑30, 47, ⬛Powell-Mason) One of the
city's best-value stays, this 1906 inn is an
old-fashioned charmer with antique furnish-
ings. Bargain rooms have windows facing
the corridor; family suites accommodate up
to five. No elevator.

Hotel Bohème
Boutique Hotel $$$

(☑415-433-9111; www.hotelboheme.com; 444
Columbus Ave; r $214-275; ◉☜; ❑10, 12, 30, 41,
45) A love letter to the Beat era, with vintage
photos, parasol lights and moody 1950s color
schemes. Rooms are smallish and some face
noisy Columbus Ave – but the North Beach
neighborhood could inspire your next novel.

Argonaut Hotel
Boutique Hotel $$$

(☑415-563-0800, 800-790-1415; www.argonauthotel.
com; 495 Jefferson St; r $389-449, with view $489-
529; ✱☜☀; ❑19, 47, 49, ⬛Powell-Hyde) ⫸ Built
as a cannery in 1908, Fisherman's Wharf's
best inn has century-old wooden beams, exposed brick walls and an over-the-top nau-
tical theme that includes porthole-shaped
mirrors. Ultra-comfy beds and iPod docks are
standard, though some rooms are small and
dark – pay extra for mesmerising bay views.

Hotel Drisco
Boutique Hotel $$$

(☑415-346-2880, 800-634-7277; www.hoteldrisco.
com; 2901 Pacific Ave; r incl breakfast $375-425;
◉☜; ❑3, 24) A stately apartment-hotel
tucked between Pacific Heights mansions,
with elegant architecture, attentive service
and understated-chic room decor. At this
lofty ridgeline location, spring for city-view
rooms and taxis.

✖ Eating

Liguria Bakery
Bakery $

(☑415-421-3786; 1700 Stockton St; focaccia $4-5;
◔8am-1pm Tue-Fri, from 7am Sat; ⬛⬛; ❑8X, 30,

39, 41, 45, ⬛Powell-Mason) Bleary-eyed art stu-
dents and Italian grandmothers line up by
8am for cinnamon-raisin focaccia hot from
the 100-year-old oven, leaving 9am dawdlers
a choice of tomato or classic rosemary. Take
yours in wax paper or boxed for picnics;
cash only.

La Taqueria
Mexican $

(☑415-285-7117; 2889 Mission St; burritos $6-8;
◔11am-9pm Mon-Sat, to 8pm Sun; ⬛; ❑12, 14, 48,
49, Ⓑ24th St Mission) SF's definitive burrito has
no debatable saffron rice, spinach tortilla or
mango salsa – just perfectly grilled meats,
slow-cooked beans and classic tomatillo or
mesquite salsa wrapped in flour tortillas.

Ichi Sushi
Sushi $$

(☑415-525-4750; www.ichisushi.com; 3282
Mission St; sushi $4-8; ◔5:30-10pm Mon-Thu, to
11pm Fri & Sat; ❑14, 49, Ⓑ24th St Mission, ⓂJ)
Ichi Sushi is a sharp cut above other fish
joints. Silky, sustainably sourced fish is
sliced with a jeweler's precision, balanced
atop well-packed rice, and topped with
powerfully tangy dabs of gelled yuzu and
microscopically diced chili daikon that
make soy sauce unthinkable.

Namu Gaji
Korean, Californian $$

(☑415-431-6268; www.namusf.com; 499 Dolores St;
small plates $10-21; ◔11:30am-4pm Wed-Fri, from
10:30am Sat & Sun, 5-10pm Tue-Thu & Sun, 5-11pm Fri
& Sat; ❑22, 33, ⓂJ, Ⓑ16th St Mission) ⫸ SF's cu-
linary advantages are showcased in Namu's
Korean-inspired soul food. Menu standouts
include ultra-savory shiitake mushroom
dumplings, meltingly tender marinated beef
tongue, and a sizzling stone pot of rice with
organic vegetables, grass-fed steak and a So-
noma farm egg.

Cotogna
Italian $$

(☑415-775-8508; www.cotognasf.com; 490 Pacific
Ave; mains $17-29; ◔11:30am-11pm Mon-Thu, 11:30am-
midnight Fri & Sat, 5-9:30pm Sun; ⬛; ❑10, 12) Rustic
Italian pastas, wood-fired pizzas and rotis-
serie meats spiked with rooftop-grown herbs
show chef Michael Tusk's finesse with well-
chosen, balanced ingredients. Book ahead or
plan a late lunch.

Outerlands
Californian $$

(☑415-661-6140; www.outerlandssf.com; 4001
Judah St; sandwiches & small plates $7-14, mains
$18-22; ◔10am-3pm Tue-Fri, from 9am Sat & Sun,
5:30-10pm Tue-Sun; ⬛; ❑18, ⓂN) ⫸ When
windy Ocean Beach leaves you feeling

Ferry Building Farmers Market
IZZET KERIBAR / GETTY IMAGES ©

shipwrecked, drift into this beach-shack bistro for organic, seed-to-table California comfort food. Brunch demands Dutch pancakes in iron skillets with housemade ricotta, and lunch brings grilled artisan-cheese combos with farm-inspired soup. Reserve ahead or enjoy wine while you wait.

Greens
Vegetarian, Californian $$

(415-771-6222; www.greensrestaurant.com; Bldg A, Fort Mason Center, cnr Marina Blvd & Laguna St; lunch $15-18, dinner $18-25; 11:45am-2:30pm & 5:30-9pm Tue-Fri, from 11am Sat, 10:30am-2pm & 5:30-9pm Sun, 5:30-9pm Mon; 28) Career carnivores won't realize there's zero meat in hearty roasted-eggplant panini and black-bean chili with crème fraîche and pickled jalapeños – they're packed with flavor-bursting ingredients grown on a Zen farm in Marin. Make reservations on weekends, or get take-out to enjoy on a wharfside bench.

Coi
Californian $$$

(415-393-9000; www.coirestaurant.com; 373 Broadway; set menu $195; 5:30-10pm Tue-Sat; 8X, 30, 41, 45, Powell-Mason) Chef Daniel Patterson's restlessly imaginative eight-course tasting menu is like licking California's coastline: rooftop-raised pansies grace Sonoma duck's tongue, and wild-caught abalone surfaces in pea-shoot tidepools. Settle in among the shaggy cushions and spot-lit stoneware to enjoy

only-in-California wine pairings ($115; generous enough for two).

Gary Danko
Californian $$$

(415-749-2060; www.garydanko.com; 800 North Point St; 3-/5-course menu $76/111; 5:30-10pm; 19, 30, 47, Powell-Hyde) The true test of SF romance is whether you're willing to share Gary Danko's crèmes brûlée trio. Smoked-glass windows prevent passersby from tripping over their tongues at roast lobster with trumpet mushrooms, duck breast with rhubarb compote, and the lavish cheese cart. Reservations required.

Benu
Californian, Fusion $$$

(415-685-4860; www.benusf.com; 22 Hawthorne St; tasting menu $195; 5:30-8:30pm Tue-Sat; 10, 12, 14, 30, 45) SF has refined fusion cuisine over 150 years, but no one rocks it quite like chef/owner Corey Lee (formerly of Napa's French Laundry), who remixes local, sustainable, fine-dining staples and Pacific Rim flavors with a SoMa DJ's finesse. Dungeness crab and truffle bring such outsize flavor to his faux-shark's-fin soup, you'll swear there's Jaws in there.

Frances
Californian $$$

(415-621-3870; www.frances-sf.com; 3870 17th St; mains $20-27; 5-10pm Sun-Thu, to 10:30pm Fri & Sat; Castro) Chef/owner Melissa Perello ditched downtown fine dining to start this bistro showcasing bright, seasonal flavors and luxurious textures: cloud-like sheep's-milk ricotta gnocchi with crunchy broccolini, grilled calamari with preserved Meyer lemon, and artisan wine served by the ounce, directly from Wine Country.

Rich Table
Californian $$$

(415-355-9085; http://richtablesf.com; 199 Gough St; meals $17-30; 5:30-10pm Sun-Thu, to 10:30pm Fri & Sat; 5, 6, 21, 47, 49, 71, Van Ness) Licking plates is the obvious move after finishing chilled apricot soup with pancetta or rabbit cannelloni with nasturtium cream. Married co-chefs/co-owners Sarah and Evan Rich invent playful, exquisite Californian food like the Dirty Hippie: silky goat-buttermilk pannacotta topped with nutty sunflower seeds and hemp. Book two to four weeks ahead (call the restaurant directly) or arrive early for bar seating.

Jardinière
Californian $$$

(☑ 415-861-5555; www.jardiniere.com; 300 Grove St; mains $18-32; ⊙ 5-10:30pm Tue-Sat, to 10pm Sun & Mon; ☐ 5, 21, 47, 49, Ⓜ Van Ness) *✦ Iron Chef, Top Chef* Master and James Beard Award-winner Traci Des Jardins champions sustainable, salacious California cuisine. She lavishes housemade tagliatelle with bone marrow and tops velvety scallops with satiny sea urchin. Go Mondays, when $55 scores three decadent courses with wine pairings.

Aziza
Moroccan, Californian $$$

(☑ 415-752-2222; www.aziza-sf.com; 5800 Geary Blvd; mains $19-29; ⊙ 5:30-10:30pm Wed-Mon; ☐ 1, 29, 31, 38) *Iron Chef* champ Mourad Lahlou's inspiration is Moroccan and his ingredients organic Californian, but the flavors are out of this world: Sonoma duck confit and caramelized onion fill flaky pastry *basteeya*, and slow-cooked Marin lamb tops saffron-infused barley. Pastry chef Melissa Chou's apricot bavarian is a goodnight kiss.

🍷 Drinking & Nightlife

Rickhouse
Bar

(☑ 415-398-2827; www.rickhousebar.com; 246 Kearny St; ⊙ 5pm-2am Mon, 3pm-2am Tue-Fri, 6pm-2am Sat; Ⓜ Montgomery, Ⓑ Montgomery) Like a shotgun shack plunked downtown, Rickhouse is lined with bourbon casks and shelving from an Ozark Mountains nunnery that once secretly brewed hooch. The emphasis is on rare bourbon, but groups guzzle authentic Pisco Punch by the garage-sale punchbowl.

Caffe Trieste
Cafe

(☑ 415-392-6739; www.caffetrieste.com; 601 Vallejo St; ⊙ 6:30am-11pm Sun-Thu, to midnight Fri & Sat; 🛜; ☐ 8X, 10, 12, 30, 41, 45) Poetry on bathroom walls, opera on the jukebox, live accordion jams weekly and sightings of Beat poet laureate Lawrence Ferlinghetti: Trieste has been a North Beach landmark since the 1950s. Sip espresso under the Sicilian mural, where Francis Ford Coppola drafted *The Godfather*. Cash only.

⭐ DON'T MISS: FERRY BUILDING

San Francisco's monument to food, the Ferry Building (☑ 415-983-8000; www.ferry-buildingmarketplace.com; Market St & the Embarcadero; ⊙ 10am-6pm Mon-Fri, 9am-6pm Sat, 11am-5pm Sun; Ⓟ ♿; Ⓜ Embarcadero, Ⓑ Embarcadero) still doubles as a trans-bay transit hub – but with dining options like these, you may never leave.

Ferry Plaza Farmers Market (☑ 415-291-3276; www.cuesa.org; Market St & the Embarcadero; ⊙ 10am-2pm Tue & Thu, 8am-2pm Sat; Ⓜ Embarcadero, Ⓑ Embarcadero) Star chefs troll farmers-market stalls for rare heirloom varietals, foodie babies blissfully teethe on organic apricots, and organic tamale trucks have rock-star fan bases. Pass time in line exchanging recipe tips, then haul your picnic to Pier 2.

Slanted Door (☑ 415-861-8032; www.slanteddoor.com; 1 Ferry Bldg; lunch $16-36, dinner $18-45; ⊙ 11am-4:30pm & 5:30-10pm Mon-Sat, 11:30am-4:30pm & 5:30-10pm Sun; Ⓜ Embarcadero, Ⓑ Embarcadero) Charles Phan earns his 2014 James Beard Outstanding Chef title with California-fresh, Vietnamese-inspired fare that rivals the sparkling Bay views – especially five-spice duck with figs. Reserve ahead or hit the takeout window.

Hog Island Oyster Company (☑ 415-391-7117; www.hogislandoysters.com; 1 Ferry Bldg; 4 oysters $13; ⊙ 11:30am-9pm Mon-Thu, to 10pm Fri, 11am-10pm Sat, 11am-9pm Sun; Ⓜ Embarcadero, Ⓑ Embarcadero) *✦* Slurp sustainably farmed Tomales Bay oysters as you please: drizzled with tangy caper buerre blanc, spiked with bacon and paprika, or au naturel with Sonoma bubbly.

Mijita (☑ 415-399-0814; www.mijitasf.com; 1 Ferry Bldg; dishes $4-10; ⊙ 10am-7pm Mon-Thu, to 8pm Fri, 9am-8pm Sat, 8:30am-3pm Sun; *✦* ♿; Ⓜ Embarcadero, Ⓑ Embarcadero) Sustainable fish tacos reign supreme and *agua fresca* (fruit punch) is made with fresh juice at chef-owner Traci des Jardin's bayfront Cal-Mex joint.

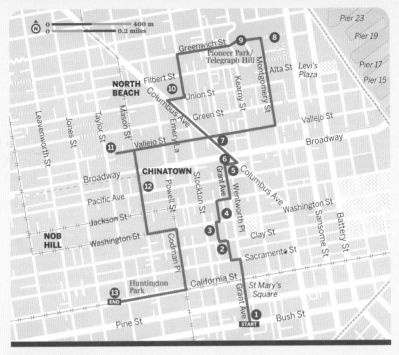

City Walk
San Francisco Hilltops

START DRAGON GATE
FINISH GRACE CATHEDRAL
LENGTH 2.3 MILES; 2½ HOURS

Conquer San Francisco's three most famous hills – Telegraph, Russian and Nob – for views that are pure poetry.

Enter Chinatown's **1 Dragon Gate** and walk up dragon-lantern-lined Grant Ave to Sacramento St. Turn left half a block up, then right onto **2 Waverly Place**, where prayer flags grace painted temple balconies. At Clay St, jog left and right again onto **3 Spofford Alley**, where Sun Yat-sen plotted revolution. At the end of the block on Washington, take a right and an immediate left onto mural-lined **4 Ross Alley**, once San Francisco's bordello byway.

Turn right down Jackson to Grant, then turn right onto **5 Jack Kerouac Alley**, where the pavement echoes Kerouac's ode to San Francisco: 'The air was soft, the stars so fine, and the promise of every cobbled alley so great...' Ahead is literary landmark **6 City Lights**, where you'll pause to read a poem upstairs in the designated Poet's Chair.

Head left up Columbus and veer right up Vallejo to fuel up with an espresso at **7 Caffe Trieste**, where Francis Ford Coppola drafted his script for *The Godfather*. Continue up Vallejo and scale the steps to Montgomery St. Go left three blocks, and turn left onto cottage-lined **8 Greenwich Street Steps** to summit Telegraph Hill. Inside **9 Coit Tower**, enjoy 1934 city views in newly restored murals downstairs and panoramic Bay views up top.

Head downhill, past wild parrots and tai-chi masters at **10 Washington Square**. Turn left on Columbus, right on Vallejo, and up three blocks to take another picturesque stairway path to flower-lined **11 Ina Coolbrith Park**. Any breath you have left will be taken away by sweeping views to Alcatraz. Summit your last hill of the day the easy way: catch the **12 Powell-Mason cable car** up Nob Hill to walk the meditation labyrinth at **13 Grace Cathedral**.

Comstock Saloon
Bar

(☑ 415-617-0071; www.comstocksaloon.com; 155 Columbus Ave; ⊙ noon to 2am Mon-Fri, from 4pm Sat, 4pm-midnight Sun; ▣ 8X, 10, 12, 30, 45, ⊠ Powell-Mason) Cocktails at this Victorian saloon remain period-perfect: Pisco Punch is made with pineapple gum and martini-precursor Martinez features gin, vermouth, bitters and maraschino liqueur.

Bar Agricole
Bar

(☑ 415-355-9400; www.baragricole.com; 355 11th St; ⊙ 6-10pm Tue-Thu & Sun, 5:30-11pm Fri & Sat; ▣ 9, 12, 27, 47) Drink your way to a history degree with these cocktails: Bellamy Scotch Sour with egg whites passes the test, but Tequila Fix with lime, pineapple gum and hellfire bitters earns honors. Don't miss the sea-urchin deviled eggs.

Smuggler's Cove
Bar

(☑ 415-869-1900; www.smugglerscovesf.com; 650 Gough St; ⊙ 5pm-1:15am; ▣ 5, 21, 49, ⊠ Van Ness) Yo-ho-ho and a bottle of rum...or perhaps a Dead Reckoning with bitters, Nicaraguan rum, tawny port and vanilla liqueur. Pirates are bedeviled by choice at this shipwreck tiki speakeasy – with 400 rums and 70 cocktails, you won't be dry-docked long.

Toronado
Pub

(☑ 415-863-2276; www.toronado.com; 547 Haight St; ⊙ 11:30am-2am; ▣ 6, 22, 71, ⊠ N) Glory hallelujah, beer lovers: your prayers are answered with 50-plus brews on tap and hundreds more bottled. Bring cash and pair seasonal ales with sausages from Rosamunde (☑ 415-437-6851; http://rosamundesausagegrill.com; 545 Haight St; sausages $6.50-7; ⊙ 11:30am-10pm Sun-Wed, to 11pm Thu-Sat; ▣ 6, 22, 71, ⊠ N) next door – it may get too loud to hear your date, but you'll hear angels sing.

- - - - - - - - - - - - - - - - - - - -

☆ Entertainment

SFJAZZ Center
Jazz

(☑ 866-920-5299; www.sfjazz.org; 201 Franklin St; ⊙ showtimes vary; ▣ 5, 7, 21, ⊠ Van Ness) America's newest, largest jazz center draws legendary artists-in-residence like Wynton Marsalis, Regina Carter and Tony Bennett (who left his heart here, after all) – but the real thrills are experimental performances, like pianist Jason Moran's jam session with SF skateboarders pounding a ramp inside the auditorium. Upper-tier cheap seats are more like stools, but offer clear stage views and ledges for drinks.

❶ Getting Around

For Bay Area transit options, departures and arrivals, check ☑ 511 or www.511.org.

BART

Bay Area Rapid Transit (www.bart.gov; one way $8.25) links San Francisco International Airport (SFO), the Mission, downtown and the East Bay. Within SF, one-way fares start at $1.75.

BICYCLE

Bicycling is safest in Golden Gate Park and along the waterfront; rentals are readily available.

CAR

Avoid driving in San Francisco: street parking is rare and meter readers ruthless. Convenient downtown parking lots are at 5th and Mission Sts, Union Sq, and Sutter and Stockton Sts. Daily rates run $25 to $50.

If your car is towed for parking violations, retrieve it from **Autoreturn** (☑ 415-865-8200; www.autoreturn.com; 450 7th St, SoMa; ⊙ 24hr; ⊠ 27, 42). Fines run to $73, plus towing and storage ($453.75 for the first four hours).

Members of **American Automobile Association** (AAA; ☑ 800-222-4357, 415-773-1900; www.aaa.com; 160 Sutter St; ⊙ 8:30am-5:30pm Mon-Fri) can call anytime for emergency service.

MUNI

MUNI (Municipal Transit Agency; www.sfmuni.com) operates bus, streetcar and cable-car lines. The standard fare for buses or streetcars is $2, and tickets are good for transfers for 90 minutes; hang onto your ticket to avoid a $100 fine. The cable-car fare is $6 per ride.

MUNI Passport (1-/3-/7-days $14/22/28) allows unlimited travel on all MUNI transport, including cable cars; it's sold at San Francisco Visitor Information Center and many hotels.

Key routes include:

California cable car California St between Market St and Van Ness Ave
F Fisherman's Wharf to Castro
J Downtown to Mission
K, L, M Downtown to Castro
N Caltrain to Haight and Ocean Beach
Powell-Mason and **Powell-Hyde cable cars** Powell and Market Sts to Fisherman's Wharf
T Embarcadero to Caltrain.

Northern Coast & Redwoods

The jagged edge of the continent is wild, scenic and even slightly foreboding, where spectral fog and an outsider spirit have fostered the world's tallest trees and a string of idiosyncratic two-stoplight towns.

Mendocino

Leading out to a gorgeous headland, Mendocino is the North Coast's salt-washed perfect village, with B&Bs surrounded by rose gardens, white-picket fences and New England–style redwood water towers. Bay Area weekenders walk along the headland among berry bramble and wildflowers, where cypress trees stand over dizzying cliffs. Nature's power is evident everywhere, from driftwood-littered fields and cave tunnels to the raging surf.

👁 Sights

Mendocino is lined with all kinds of interesting galleries, which hold openings on the second Saturday of each month from 5pm to 8pm.

Mendocino Art Center   Gallery
(📞707-937-5818, 800 653 3328; www.mendocino artcenter.org; 45200 Little Lake St; ⊘10am-5pm Apr-Oct, to 4pm Tue-Sat Nov-Mar) Behind a yard of twisting iron sculpture, the city's art center takes up a whole tree-filled block, hosting exhibitions, the 81-seat Helen Schonei Theatre and nationally renowned art classes. This is also where to pick up the *Mendocino Arts Showcase* brochure, a quarterly publication listing all the happenings and festivals in town.

Point Cabrillo Lighthouse   Lighthouse
(www.pointcabrillo.org; Point Cabrillo Dr; ⊘11am-4pm Sat & Sun Jan & Feb, daily Mar-Oct, Fri-Mon Nov &

Dec) FREE Restored in 1909, this stout lighthouse stands on a 300-acre wildlife preserve north of town, between Russian Gulch and Caspar Beach. Guided walks of the preserve leave at 11am on Sundays from May to September. You can also stay in the lighthouse keeper's house and cottages which are now vacation rentals.

🏃 Activities

Wine tours, whale-watching, shopping, hiking, cycling: there's more to do in the area than a thousand long weekends could accomplish. For navigable river and ocean kayaking, launch from tiny Albion, which hugs the north side of the Albion River mouth, 5 miles south of Mendocino.

Catch A Canoe &
Bicycles Too!   Canoeing, Kayaking
(📞707-937-0273; www.catchacanoe.com; Stanford Inn by the Sea, 44850 Comptche-Ukiah Rd; kayak & canoe rental adult/child from $28/14; ⊘9am-5pm) This friendly outfit at the Stanford Inn south of town rents bikes, kayaks and stable outrigger canoes for trips up the 8-mile Big River tidal estuary, the longest undeveloped estuary in Northern California. No highways or buildings, only beaches, forests, marshes, streams, abundant wildlife and historic logging sites. Bring a picnic and a camera to enjoy the ramshackle remnants of century-old train trestles and majestic blue herons.

🛏 Sleeping

Standards are high and so are prices; two-day minimums often crop up on weekends. Fort Bragg (p68), 10 miles north, has cheaper lodgings. All B&B rates include breakfast; only a few places have TVs. For a range of cottages and B&Bs, contact Mendocino Coast Reservations (☏ 800-262-7801, 707-937-5033; www.mendocinovacations.com; 45084 Little Lake St; ⏱ 9am-5pm).

Russian Gulch State Park   Campground $

(☏ reservations 800-444-7275; www.reserveamerica.com; tent & RV sites $35) In a wooded canyon 2 miles north of town, with secluded drive-in sites, hot showers, a small waterfall and the Devil's Punch Bowl (a collapsed sea arch).

Andiron   Cabin $$

(☏ 800-955-6478, 707-937-1543; http://theandiron.com; 6051 N Hwy 1, Little River; most cabins $109-299; 🐾🛝) 🌿 Styled with hip vintage decor, this cluster of 1950s roadside cottages is a refreshingly playful option amid the cabbage-rose and lace aesthetic of Mendocino. Each cabin houses two rooms with complementing themes: 'Read' has old books, comfy vintage chairs and hip retro eyeglasses, while the adjoining 'Write' features a huge chalk board and a ribbon typewriter.

Alegria   B&B $$$

(☏ 800-780-7905, 707-937-5150; www.oceanfrontmagic.com; 44781 Main St; r $239-299; 🐾) A perfect romantic hideaway, beds have views over the coast, decks have ocean views and all rooms have wood-burning fireplaces. Outside a gorgeous path leads to a big, amber-grey beach. Ever-so-friendly innkeepers whip up amazing breakfasts served in the sea-view dining area. Less expensive rooms are available across the street at bright and simple Raku House (www.rakuhouse.com; r from $159).

Mendocino Hotel   Historic Hotel $$$

(☏ 800-548-0513, 707-937-0511; www.mendocinohotel.com; 45080 Main St; r with/without bath from $261/186, ste $475; 🅿🐾) Built in 1878 as the town's first hotel, this is like a piece of the Old West. The modern garden suites sit behind the main building and don't have a shade of old-school class, but are modern and serviceable. As gorgeous as it is, the prices are inflated, especially for the rooms with shared bathrooms.

🍴 Eating

With quality to rival Napa Valley, the influx of Bay Area weekenders have fostered an excellent dining scene that enthusiastically espouses organic, sustainable principles. Make reservations. Gathering picnic supplies is easy at Mendosa's (☏ 8am-9pm; www.harvestmarket.com; 10501 Lansing St) 🌿 organic grocery store (with deli) and the farmers market (cnr Howard & Main St; ⏱ noon-2pm Fri May-Oct).

GoodLife Cafe & Bakery   Cafe $

(http://goodlifecafemendo.com; 10485 Lansing St; light meals $6-10; ⏱ 8am-4pm) 🌿 Here's where locals and tourists mingle in an unpretentious, noisy and cozy cafe setting. Get bakery goods and fair-trade coffee for breakfast and comfort food like mac and cheese or curry bowls at lunch. Lots of gluten-free options are available.

Mendocino Market   Deli $

(45051 Ukiah St; sandwiches $6-9; ⏱ 11am-5pm Mon-Fri, to 4pm Sat & Sun; 🐾) Pick up huge deli sandwiches and picnics here.

Mendocino Cafe   Californian, Fusion $$

(www.mendocinocafe.com; 10451 Lansing St; lunch mains $12-16, dinner mains $21-33; ⏱ 11:30am-8pm; 🐾) One of Mendocino's few fine dinner spots that also serves lovely alfresco lunches on its ocean-view deck surrounded by roses. Try the fish tacos or the 'Healing Bowl' of soba noodles, miso, shitake mushrooms and choice of meat or seafood. At dinner there's grilled steak and seafood.

★ Café Beaujolais   Californian $$$

(☏ 707-937-5614; www.cafebeaujolais.com; 961 Ukiah St; dinner mains $23-35; ⏱ 11:30am-2:30pm Wed-Sun, dinner from 5:30pm daily) 🌿 Mendocino's iconic, beloved country-Cal–French restaurant occupies an 1896 house restyled into a monochromatic urban-chic dining room, perfect for holding hands by candlelight. The refined, inspired cooking draws diners from San Francisco, who make this the centerpiece of their trip. The locally sourced menu changes with the seasons, but the Petaluma duck breast served with crispy skin is a gourmand's delight.

🍷 Drinking & Nightlife

Have cocktails at the Mendocino Hotel or the Grey Whale Bar at the MacCallum House

Restaurant. For boisterousness and beer head straight to **Patterson's Pub**.

Dick's Place
Dive Bar

(45080 Main St) A bit out of place among the fancy-pants shops downtown, but an excellent spot to check out the *other* Mendocino and do shots with rowdy locals.

❶ Information

Ford House Museum & Visitor Center (☑ 707-537-5397; http://mendoparks.org; 735 Main St; ⊙ 11am-4pm) Maps, books, information and exhibits, including a scale model of 1890 Mendocino.

Fort Bragg

In the past, Fort Bragg was Mendocino's ugly stepsister, home to a lumber mill, a scrappy downtown and blue-collar locals who gave a cold welcome to outsiders. Since the mill closure in 2002, the town has started to reinvent itself, slowly warming to a tourism-based economy.

◉ Sights & Activities

Fort Bragg has the same banner North Coast activities as Mendocino – beach combing, surfing, hiking – but basing yourself here is much cheaper and arguably less quaint and pretentious. The wharf lies at Noyo Harbor – the mouth of the Noyo River – south of downtown where you can find **whale-watching cruises** and **deep-sea fishing trips**.

Mendocino Coast Botanical Gardens
Gardens

(☑ 707-964-4352; www.gardenbythesea.org; 18220 N Hwy 1; adult/child/senior $14/5/10; ⊙ 9am-5pm Mar-Oct, to 4pm Nov-Feb) 🦽 This gem of Northern California displays native flora, rhododendrons and heritage roses. The succulent display alone is amazing and the organic garden is harvested by volunteers to feed area residents in need. The serpentine paths wander along 47 seafront acres south of town. Primary trails are wheelchair-accessible.

Glass Beach
Beach

Named for (what's left of) the sea-polished glass in the sand, remnants of its days as a city dump, this beach is now part of MacKerricher State Park where visitors comb the sand for multicolored glass. Take the headlands trail from Elm St, off Main St, but leave the glass; as a part of the park system, visitors are not supposed to pocket souvenirs.

⭐ Skunk Train
Historic Train

(☑ 866-866-1690, 707-964-6371; www.skunktrain.com; adult/child $54/34; 🐾) Fort Bragg's pride and joy, the vintage train got its nickname in 1925 for its stinky gas-powered steam engines, but today the historic steam and diesel locomotives are odorless. Passing through redwood-forested mountains, along rivers, over bridges and through deep mountain tunnels, the trains run from both Fort Bragg and Willits to the midway point of Northspur, where they turn around.

All-Aboard Adventures
Fishing, Whale-Watching

(☑ 707-964-1881; www.allaboardadventures.com; 32400 N Harbor Dr) Captain Tim leads crabbing and salmon-fishing trips (five hours, $80) and whale-watching during the whale migration (two hours, $35).

⛏ Sleeping

Fort Bragg's lodging is cheaper than Mendocino's, but most of the motels along noisy Hwy 1 don't have air-conditioning, so you'll hear traffic through your windows. Most B&Bs do not have TVs and they all include breakfast. The usual chains abound. The best-value bland motel is **Colombi Motel** (☑ 707-964-5773; www.colombimotel.com; 647 Oak St; 1-/2-bedroom units with kitchenette from $60/70; 🛜) which is in town, not on the highway.

Country Inn
B&B $

(☑ 707-964-3737; www.beourguests.com; 632 N Main St; r $80-220; 🛜🐾) This cute-as-a-button, gingerbread-trimmed B&B is right in the middle of town and is an excellent way to dodge the chain motels for a good-value stay. The lovely family hosts are welcoming and easygoing, and can offer good local tips. Breakfast can be delivered to your room and at night you can soak in a hot tub out back.

California Department of Forestry
Campground $

(☑ 707-964-5674; 802 N Main St; ⊙ 8am-4:30pm Mon, to noon Tue-Thu) Come here for maps, permits and camping information for the **Jackson State Forest**, east of Fort Bragg, where camping is free – which attracts all sorts so this isn't recommended for families or solo women.

Shoreline Cottages
Motel, Cottage $$

(☑ 707-964-2977; www.shoreline-cottage.com; 18725 Shoreline Hwy, Fort Bragg; d $95-165; 🛜🐾) Low-key, four-person rooms and cottages with kitchens surround a central, tree-filled lawn.

The family rooms are a good bargain, and suites feature modern artwork and clean sight lines. All rooms have docks for your iPod, snacks and access to a library of DVDs and there's a communal hot tub.

Weller House Inn   B&B $$$

(☑877-893-5537, 707-964-4415; www.wellerhouse. com; 524 Stewart St; r $200-310; ☎) Rooms in this beautifully restored 1886 mansion have down comforters, good mattresses and fine linens. The water tower is the tallest structure in town – and it has a hot tub at the top! Breakfast is in the massive redwood ballroom.

✗ Eating

Similar to the lodging scene, the food in Fort Bragg is less spendy than Mendocino, but there are a number of truly excellent options. Self-caterers should try the **farmers market** (cnr Laurel & Franklin Sts; ☉3:30-6pm Wed May-Oct) downtown or the **Harvest Market** (☑707-964-7000; cnr Hwys 1 & 20; ☉5am-11pm) for the best groceries.

Los Gallitos   Mexican $

(130 S Main St; burritos $5.25-6.25; ☉11am-8pm Mon-Sat, from 10am Sun) A packed hole-in-the-wall that serves the best Mexican on the coast. Chips are homemade, the guacamole is chunky and the dishes, from the fresh fish tacos to homemade pork tamales and generous *sopas*, are consistently flavorful and well beyond the standard glob of refried beans. It's located across the parking lot from the CVS.

Headlands Coffeehouse   Cafe $

(www.headlandscoffeehouse.com; 120 E Laurel St; dishes $4-8; ☉7am-10pm Mon-Sat, to 7pm Sun; ☎�) The town's best cafe is in the middle of the historic downtown, with high ceilings and lots of atmosphere. The menu gets raves for the Belgian waffles, homemade soups, veggie-friendly salads, panini and lasagna.

★Piaci Pub & Pizzeria   Italian $$

(www.piacipizza.com; 120 W Redwood Ave; mains $8-18; ☉11am-9:30pm Mon-Thu, to 10pm Fri & Sat, 4-9:30pm Sun) Fort Bragg's must-visit pizzeria is known for its sophisticated wood-fired, brick-oven pies as much as for its long list of microbrews. Try the 'Gustoso' – with chèvre, pesto and seasonal pears – all carefully orchestrated on a thin crust. It's tiny, loud and fun, with much more of a bar atmosphere than a restaurant. Expect to wait at peak times.

Point Cabrillo lighthouse (p66)
THOMAS WINZ / GETTY IMAGES ©

North Coast Brewing Company   Brewery $$

(www.northcoastbrewing.com; 455 N Main St; mains $8-25; ☉7am-9:30pm Sun-Thu, to 10pm Fri & Sat) Though thick, rare slabs of steak and a list of specials demonstrate that they take the food as seriously as the bevvies, it's burgers and garlic fries that soak up the fantastic selection of handcrafted brews. A great stop for serious beer lovers.

❶ Getting Around

Fort Bragg Cyclery (☑707-964-3509; www. fortbraggcyclery.com; 221a N Main St; bike rental per day from $32) Rents bicycles.

Eureka

One hour north of Garberville, on the edge of the giant Humboldt Bay, lies Eureka, the largest bay north of San Francisco. With strip-mall sprawl surrounding a lovely historic downtown, it wears its role as the county seat a bit clumsily.

◉ Sights

The free *Eureka Visitors Map*, available at tourist offices, details walking tours and scenic drives, focusing on architecture and history. **Old Town**, along 2nd and 3rd Sts from C St to M St, was once down-and-out, but has been refurbished into a buzzing pedestrian district. The F Street Plaza and Boardwalk run along the waterfront at the foot of F St. Gallery openings fall on the first Saturday of every month.

Blue Ox Millworks &
Historic Park   Historic Building
See p26.

Carson Mansion   Historic Building
See p26.

🕊 Activities

Harbor Cruise   Cruise
See p26.

Hum-Boats Sail, Canoe &
Kayak Center   Boat Rental
(www.humboats.com; Startare Dr; ⊙9am-5pm Mon-Fri, to 6pm Sat & Sun Apr-Oct, to 2:30pm Nov-Mar) At Woodley Island Marina, this outfit rents kayaks and sailboats, offering lessons, tours, charters, sunset sails and full-moon paddles.

🛏 Sleeping

Every brand of chain hotel is along Hwy 101. Room rates run high midsummer; you can sometimes find cheaper in Arcata, to the north, or Fortuna, to the south. There are also a handful of motels which cost from $55 to $100 and have no air-conditioning; choose places set back from the road. The cheapest are south of downtown on the suburban strip.

Abigail's Elegant Victorian Mansion   Inn $$
(☑707-444-3144; www.eureka-california.com; 1406 C St; r $115-450; 🐾) Inside this National Historic Landmark that's practically a living-history museum, the sweet-as-could-be innkeepers lavish guests with warm hospitality.

Eureka Inn   Historic Hotel $$
(☑877-552-3985, 707-497-6903; www.eurekainn.com; cnr 7th & F Sts; r from $109; 🐾) This magestic and enormous historic hotel is slowly being renovated. The style is cozy, in an early-20th-century-lodger, vaguely Wild West sort of way. The staff are extremely friendly and there's a decent bar and restaurant on the premises.

🍴 Eating

Eureka is blessed with two excellent natural food grocery stores – Eureka Co-op (cnr 5th & L Sts) and Eureka Natural Foods (1626 Broadway) – and two weekly farmers markets

(cnr 2nd & F Sts; ⊙10am-1pm Tue Jun-Oct) and the Henderson Center (⊙10am-1pm Thu Jun-Oct). The vibrant dining scene is focused in the Old Town district.

Ramone's   Bakery, Deli $
(2223 Harrison St; mains $6-10; ⊙7am-6pm Mon-Sat, 8am-4pm Sun) For grab-and-go sandwiches, fresh soups and wraps.

Brick & Fire   Californian $$
(☑707-268-8959; 1630 F St; pizzas from $14, mains $15-25; ⊙11:30am-8:30pm Mon, Wed & Thu, 11:30am-9pm Fri, 5-9pm Sat & Sun) Eureka's best restaurant is in an intimate, warm-hued, bohemian-tinged setting that is almost always busy. Choose from thin-crust pizzas, delicious salads (try the pear and blue cheese) and an ever-changing selection of appetizers and mains that highlight local produce and wild mushrooms. There's a weighty wine list and servers are well-versed in pairings.

🍸 Drinking & Nightlife

Lost Coast Brewery   Brewery
(☑707-445-4480; 617 4th St; 10 tasters for $12; ⊙11am-10pm Sun-Thu, to 11pm Fri & Sat; 🐾) The roster of the regular brews at Eureka's colorful brewery might not knock the socks off a serious beer snob (and can't hold a candle to some of the others on the coast), but highlights include the Downtown Brown Ale, Great White and Lost Coast Pale Ale. After downing a few pints, the fried pub grub starts to look pretty tasty.

ℹ Information

Eureka Chamber of Commerce (☑800-356-6381, 707-442-3738; www.eurekachamber.com; 2112 Broadway; ⊙8:30am-5pm Mon-Fri; 🐾) The main visitor information center is on Hwy 101.

Six Rivers National Forest Headquarters (☑707-442-1721; 1330 Bayshore Way; ⊙8am-4:30pm Mon-Fri) Maps and information.

Trinidad

Cheery, tiny Trinidad perches prettily on the side of the ocean, combining upscale homes with a mellow surfer vibe.

👁 Sights & Activities

Trinidad is small: approach via Hwy 101 or from the north via Patrick's Point Dr (which becomes Scenic Dr further south). To reach town, take Main St.

The free town map at the information kiosk shows several fantastic hiking trails, most notably the Trinidad Head Trail (see p30) with superb coastal views; excellent for whale-watching (December to April). Stroll along an exceptionally beautiful cove at Trinidad State Beach; take Main St and bear right at Stagecoach, then take the second turn left (the first is a picnic area) into the small lot.

Scenic Dr twists south along coastal bluffs, passing tiny coves with views back toward the bay. It peters out before reaching the broad expanses of Luffenholtz Beach (accessible via the staircase) and serene white-sand Moonstone Beach. Exit Hwy 101 at 6th Ave/Westhaven to get there. Further south Moonstone becomes Clam Beach County Park.

Surfing is good year-round, but potentially dangerous: unless you know how to judge conditions and get yourself out of trouble – there are no lifeguards here – surf in better-protected Crescent City.

🛏 Sleeping

Many of the inns line Patrick's Point Dr, north of town. Trinidad Retreats (www.trinidadretreats. com) and Redwood Coast Vacation Rentals (www.redwoodcoastvacationrentals.com) handle local property rentals.

Clam Beach Campground $

(tent sites per car $15) South of town off Hwy 101, this beach has excellent camping, but can get crowded and it's a favorite with traveling homeless. Pitch your tent in the dunes (look for natural windbreaks). Facilities include pit toilets, cold water, picnic tables and fire rings.

View Crest Lodge Lodge $$

(☑707-677-3393; www.viewcrestlodge.com; 3415 Patrick's Point Dr; sites $27, 1-bedroom cottages $95-240; 🐾) On a hill above the ocean on the inland side, some of the well-maintained, modern and terrific-value cottages have views and Jacuzzis; most have kitchens. There's also a good campground.

★Trinidad Bay B&B B&B $$$

(☑707-677-0840; www.trinidadbaybnb.com; 560 Edwards St; r incl breakfast $200-300; 🐾) Opposite the lighthouse, this gorgeous light-filled Cape Cod–style place overlooks the harbor and Trinidad Head. Breakfast is delivered to your uniquely styled room and in the after-noon the house fills with the scent of freshly baked cookies. The Trinity Alps room has a kitchenette and is well-set up for families.

🍴 Eating & Drinking

Lighthouse Café Fast Food $

(☑707-677-0390; 355 Main St; mains $6-9; ⊙11am-7pm Tue-Sun; 🐾) 🍴 Across from the Chevron, this fun little arty joint makes good food fast, using mostly organic ingredients – try the creative soups, fish and chips with hand-cut fries, local grass-fed beef burgers and homemade ice creams. Order at the counter and then sit inside or out.

The Seascape Seafood $$

(1 Bay St; mains $12-35; ⊙7am-8:30pm) Go to this old-school, diner-type place for a panoramic view of the sea more than the food. It's a lovely spot to watch the daily catch come in over a slice of pie or a bowl of yummy clam chowder.

Larrupin Cafe Californian $$$

(☑707-677-0230; www.larrupin.com; 1658 Patrick's Point Dr; mains $20-37; ⊙5-9pm) Everybody loves Larrupin, where Moroccan rugs, chocolate-brown walls, gravity-defying floral arrangements and deep-burgundy Oriental carpets create a moody atmosphere perfect for a lovers' tryst. On the menu expect consistently good mesquite-grilled seafood and meats – the smoked beef brisket is amazing. In the summer book a table on the garden patio for live music Wednesday and Friday nights.

ℹ Information

Information Kiosk (cnr Patrick's Point Dr & Main St) Just west of the freeway. The pamphlet Discover Trinidad has an excellent map.

Trinidad Chamber of Commerce (☑707-667-1610; www.trinidadcalif.com) Information on the web, but no visitor center.

Patrick's Point State Park

Coastal bluffs jut out to sea at 640-acre Patrick's Point (see p31), where sandy beaches abut rocky headlands. Five miles north of Trinidad, with supereasy access to dramatic coastal bluffs, it's a best-bet for families. Stroll scenic overlooks, climb giant rock formations, watch whales breach, gaze into tidepools, or listen to barking sea lions and singing birds from this manicured park.

Redwood forest, northern California
PATRICK ORTON / GETTY IMAGES ©

Sumêg (see p32) is an authentic reproduction of a Yurok village, with hand-hewn redwood buildings where Native Americans gather for traditional ceremonies. In the native plant garden you'll find species for making traditional baskets and medicines.

On Agate Beach look for stray bits of jade and sea-polished agate. Follow the signs to tidepools, but tread lightly and obey regulations. The 2-mile Rim Trail, a old Yurok trail around the bluffs, circles the point with access to huge rocky outcroppings. Don't miss Wedding Rock, one of the park's most romantic spots. Other trails lead around unusual formations like Ceremonial Rock and Lookout Rock.

The park's three well-tended campgrounds (☎ reservations 800-444-7275; www.reserveamerica.com; tent & RV sites $35) have coin-operated hot showers and very clean bathrooms. Penn Creek and Abalone campgrounds are more sheltered than Agate Beach.

Humboldt Lagoons State Park

See p32 for sights information.

All campsites are first-come, first-served. The park runs two environmental campgrounds (tent sites $20; ☻ Apr-Oct); bring water. Stone Lagoon has six boat-in environmental campsites. Check in at Patrick's Point State Park, at least 30 minutes before sunset.

Humboldt County Parks (☎ 707-445-7651; tent sites $20) operates a lovely cypress-grove picnic area and campground beside Big La-

goon, a mile off Hwy 101, with flush toilets and cold water, but no showers.

Redwood National Park

Just north of the southern visitor center, turn east onto Bald Hills Rd and travel 2 miles to Lady Bird Johnson Grove, one of the park's most spectacular groves, and also one of the busiest, accessible via a gentle 1-mile loop trail. Continue for another 5 miles up Bald Hills Rd to Redwood Creek Overlook. On the top of the ridgeline, at 2100ft, get views over the forest and the entire watershed – provided it's not foggy. Just past the overlook lies the gated turnoff for Tall Trees Grove, the location of several of the world's tallest trees. Rangers issue 50 vehicle permits. Pick one up, along with the gate-lock combination, from the visitor centers. Allow four hours for the round-trip, which includes a 6-mile drive down a rough dirt road (speed limit 15mph) and a steep 1.3-mile one-way hike, which descends 800ft to the grove.

Several longer trails include the awe-inspiring Redwood Creek Trail, which also reaches Tall Trees Grove. You'll need a free backcountry permit to hike and camp (highly recommended, as the best backcountry camping on the North Coast), but the area is most accessible from Memorial Day to Labor Day, when summer footbridges are up. Otherwise, getting across the creek can be perilous or impossible.

For hikes, kayaking, fishing or a slew of other tours, book with Redwood Adventures (☎ 866-733-9637; www.redwoodadventures.com; 7 Valley Green Camp Rd, Orick) whose guides know the area better than anyone and will get you to places you may not otherwise find on your own. For horseback riding from May to November call the Redwood Creek Bukarettes (☎ 707-499-2943; www.redwoodcreekbukarettes.com; 1000 Drydens Rd, Orick; 1½hr trail rides from $60).

🛏 Sleeping

Elk Meadow Cabins   Cabins $$$
(☎ 866-733-9637; www.redwoodadventures.com; 7 Valley Green Camp Rd, Orick; cabins $179-279; ☎ 🐾) These spotless and bright cabins with equipped kitchens and all the mod-cons are in a perfect mid-parks location – they're great if you're traveling in a group and the most comfy choice even if you're not. Expect to see elk on the lawn in the mornings. Cab-

ins sleep six to eight people and there's an additional $45 cleaning fee.

ℹ️ Information

Unlike most national parks, there are no fees and no highway entrance stations at Redwood National Park, so it's imperative to pick up the free map at the park headquarters in Crescent City (p73) or at the infomation center in Orick. Rangers here issue permits to visit Tall Trees Grove and loan bear-proof containers for backpackers.

For in-depth redwood ecology, buy the excellent official park handbook. The **Redwood Parks Association** (www.redwoodparksassociation.org) provides good information on its website, including detailed descriptions of all the parks hikes.

Redwood Information Center (Kuchel Visitor Center; ☑ 707-464-6101; www.nps.gov/redw; Hwy 101; ⊙ 9am-6pm June-Aug, to 5pm Sep-Oct & Mar-May, to 4pm Nov-Feb) On Hwy 101, a mile south of tiny Orick.

Del Norte Coast Redwoods State Park

Marked by steep canyons and dense woods north of Klamath, half the 6400 acres of this park (☑ 707-464-6101, ext 5120; per car day-use $8) are virgin redwood forest, crisscrossed by 15 miles of hiking trails. Even the most cynical of redwood-watchers can't help but be moved.

Pick up maps and inquire about guided walks at the Redwood National & State Parks Headquarters (☑ 707-464-6101; 1111 2nd St, Crescent City; ⊙ 9am-5pm Oct-May, to 6pm Jun-Sep) in Crescent City or the Redwood Information Center in Orick.

Hwy 1 winds in from the coast at rugged, dramatic Wilson Beach, and traverses the dense forest, with groves stretching off as far as you can see.

Picnic on the sand at False Klamath Cove. Heading north, tall trees cling precipitously to canyon walls that drop to the rocky, timber-strewn coastline, and it's almost impos-sible to get to the water, except via the gorgeous but steep Damnation Creek Trail or Footsteps Rock Trail.

Between these two, serious hikers will be most greatly rewarded by the Damnation Creek Trail. It's only 4 miles long, but the 1100-ft elevation change and cliff-side redwood makes it the park's best hike. The unmarked trailhead starts from a parking area off Hwy 101 at Mile 16.

Crescent Beach Overlook and picnic area has superb wintertime whale-watching. At the park's north end, watch the surf pound at Crescent Beach, just south of Crescent City via Enderts Beach Rd.

Mill Creek Campground (☑ 800-444-7275; www.reserveamerica.com; tent & RV sites $35) has hot showers and 145 sites in a redwood grove, 2 miles east of Hwy 101 and 7 miles south of Crescent City. Sites 1-74 are woodsier; sites 75-145 sunnier. Hike-in sites are prettiest.

Jedediah Smith Redwoods State Park

The northernmost park in the system of Redwood National & State Parks, Jedediah Smith (see p34) is 10 miles northeast of Crescent City (via Hwy 101 east to Hwy 197). Stop for a stroll under enormous trees in Simpson-Reed Grove. If it's foggy at the coast it may be sunny here. There's a swimming hole and picnic area near the park entrance. An easy half-mile trail, departing from the far side of the campground, crosses the Smith River via a summer-only footbridge, leading to Stout Grove, the park's most famous grove. The visitor center (☑ 707-464-6101; ⊙ 10am-4pm daily Jun-Aug, Sat & Sun Sep-Oct & Apr-May) sells hiking maps and nature guides. If you wade in the river, be careful in the spring when currents are swift and the water cold.

Coastal Hwy 1 pulls out all the stops, scenery-wise. Flower-power Santa Cruz and the historic port town of Monterey are gateways to the rugged wilderness of the bohemian Big Sur coast.

Central Coast

Santa Cruz

Santa Cruz has marched to its own beat since long before the Beat Generation. It's counterculture central, a touchy-feely, new-agey city famous for its leftie-liberal politics and live-and-let-live ideology – except when it comes to dogs (rarely allowed off-leash), parking (meters run seven days a week) and Republicans (allegedly shot on sight). It's still cool to be a hippie or a stoner here (or better yet, both), although some far-out-looking freaks are just slumming Silicon Valley millionaires and trust-fund babies.

- - - - - - - - - - - - - - - - - - -

◉ Sights & Activities

One of the best things to do in Santa Cruz is simply stroll, shop and watch the sideshow along Pacific Ave downtown.

Santa Cruz Beach Boardwalk Amusement Park
See p24.

Seymour Marine Discovery Center Museum
(☑ 831-459-3800; http://seymourcenter.ucsc.edu; 100 Shaffer Rd; adult/child 3-16yr $8/6; ⊙ 10am-5pm Tue-Sun year-round, also 10am-5pm Mon Jul & Aug; ♿) 🍃 By Natural Bridges State Beach, this kids' educational center is part of UCSC's Long Marine Laboratory. Interactive natural-science exhibits include tidal touch pools and aquariums, while outside you can gawk at the world's largest blue-whale skeleton.

Guided one-hour tours happen at 1pm, 2pm and 3pm daily, with a special 30-minute tour for families with younger children at 11am; sign up for tours in person an hour in advance (no reservations).

Sanctuary Exploration Center Museum
(☑ 831-421-9993; http://montereybay.noaa.gov; 35 Pacific Ave; ⊙ 10am-5pm Wed-Sun; ♿) 🍃 FREE Operated by the Monterey Bay National Marine Sanctuary, this educational museum near the beach boardwalk is an interactive multimedia experience that teaches kids and adults about the bay's marine treasures, watershed conservation and high-tech underwater exploration for scientific research.

Surfing

Year-round, water temperatures average under 60°F, meaning that without a wetsuit, body parts quickly turn blue. Surfing is incredibly popular, especially at experts-only Steamer Lane and beginners' Cowell's, both off West Cliff Dr. Other favorite surf spots include Pleasure Point Beach, on East Cliff Dr toward Capitola, and Manresa State Beach off Hwy 1 southbound.

Santa Cruz Surf School Surfing
(☑ 831-345-8875, 831-426-7072; www.santacruzsurf school.com; 131 Center St; 2hr group/1hr private lesson $90/120; ♿) Wanna learn to surf? Near the wharf, friendly male and female instructors will have you standing and surfing on your first day out.

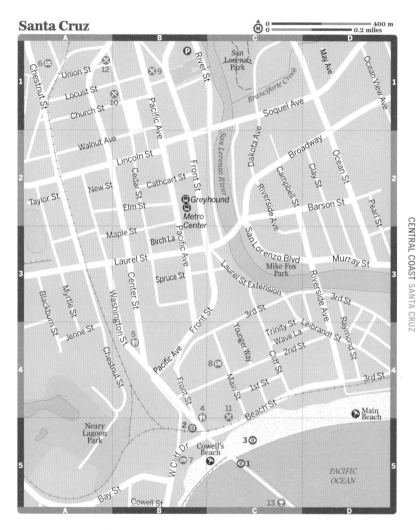

Kayaking, Whale-Watching & Fishing

Kayaking lets you discover the craggy coastline and kelp beds where sea otters float. Winter whale-watching trips run from December through April, though there's plenty of marine life to see on a summer bay cruise. Many fishing trips depart from the wharf, where a few shops rent fishing tackle and poles.

📖 Sleeping

Santa Cruz does not have enough beds to satisfy demand: expect outrageous prices at peak times for nothing-special rooms. Places near the beach boardwalk run the gamut from friendly to frightening. If you're looking for a straightforward motel, cruise Ocean St inland or Mission St (Hwy 1) near the UCSC campus.

HI Santa Cruz Hostel   Hostel $

(📞831-423-8304; www.hi-santacruz.org; 321 Main St; dm $26-29, r $60-110, all with shared bath; ⊙check-in 5-10pm; @) Budget overnighters dig this hostel at the century-old Carmelita Cottages surrounded by flowering gardens, just two blocks from the beach. Cons: midnight curfew, daytime lockout (10am

Santa Cruz

to 5pm) and three-night maximum stay. Reservations are essential. Street parking costs $2.

California State Park Campgrounds
Campground $

(🖉 reservations 800-444-7275; www.reserveamerica.com; tent & RV sites $35-65; 🐾) Book well ahead to camp at state beaches off Hwy 1 south of Santa Cruz or up in the foggy Santa Cruz Mountains off Hwy 9. Family-friendly campgrounds here include Henry Cowell Redwoods State Park in Felton as well as New Brighton State Beach in Capitola.

Adobe on Green B&B
B&B $$

(🖉 831-469-9866; www.adobeongreen.com; 103 Green St; r incl breakfast $169-219; 🛜) 🖋 Peace and quiet are the mantras at this place, a short walk from Pacific Ave. The hosts are practically invisible, but their thoughtful touches are everywhere, from boutique-hotel amenities in spacious, stylish and solar-powered rooms to breakfast spreads from their organic gardens.

Dream Inn
Hotel $$$

(🖉 866-774-7735, 831-426-4330; www.dreaminnsantacruz.com; 175 W Cliff Dr; r $249-479; ❄️@🛜🏊) Overlooking the wharf from a spectacular hillside perch, this chic boutique hotel is as stylish as Santa Cruz gets.

Rooms have all mod cons, while the beach is just steps away. Don't miss happy hour at Aquarius restaurant's ocean-view bar. Parking is $25.

🍴 Eating & Drinking

Downtown is chockablock with casual cafes. If you're looking for seafood, wander the wharf's takeout counter joints. Mission St, near UCSC, and 41st Ave offer cheaper eats.

★ Penny Ice Creamery
Ice Cream $

(www.thepennyicecreamery.com; 913 Cedar St; snacks $2-4; ⊙ noon-11pm; 🖐) 🖋 With a cult following, this artisan ice-cream shop crafts zany flavors like bourbon candied ginger, lemon verbena blueberry and ricotta apricot all from scratch using local, organic and wild-harvested ingredients. Even vanilla is special: it's made using Thomas Jefferson's original recipe. Also at a downtown kiosk (1520 Pacific Ave; ⊙ noon-6pm Sun-Thu, to 9pm Fri & Sat; 🖐) 🖋 and near Pleasure Point (820 41st Ave; ⊙ noon-9pm Sun-Thu, to 11pm Fri & Sat; 🖐) 🖋.

Pono Hawaiian Grill
Fusion $$

(www.ponohawaiiangrill.com; 120 Union St; mains $7-15; ⊙ 11am-10pm Sun-Wed, to 11pm Thu-Sat) Inside the Reef bar, this kitchen runs on 'island time' as it mixes up your fresh ahi tuna, salmon, shellfish or veggie *poke* (cubed raw salad) in a bowl or ladled on a plate with two-scoop rice and creamy macaroni or tossed green salad. The *loco moco* burrito with spicy gravy is a huge hit.

Engfer Pizza Works
Pizzeria $$

(www.engferpizzaworks.com; 537 Seabright Ave; pizzas $8-23; ⊙ usually 4-9:30pm Tue-Sun; 🖉🖐) Detour to find this old factory, where wood-fired oven pizzas are made from completely from scratch – the no-name specialty is like a giant salad on roasted bread. You can play ping-pong and down draft microbrews while you wait.

Verve Coffee Roasters
Cafe

(www.vervecoffeeroasters.com; 1540 Pacific Ave; ⊙ 6:30am-9pm; 🛜) To sip finely roasted artisan espresso or a cup of rich pour-over coffee, join the surfers and hipsters at this industrial-zen cafe. Single-origin brews and house blends rule.

Vino Prima Wine Bar

(www.vinoprimawines.com; 55 Municipal Wharf; ⊙ 2-8pm Mon-Tue, 2-10pm Wed-Fri, noon-10pm Sat, noon-8pm Sun) With dreamy ocean views, this spot pours California boutique wines, including hard-to-find bottles from around Santa Cruz and Monterey Counties.

❶ Information

Santa Cruz Visitor Center (☑ 800-833-3494, 831-429-7281; www.santacruzca.org; 303 Water St; ⊙ 9am-noon & 1-4pm Mon-Fri, 11am-3pm Sat & Sun) Free public internet terminal, maps and brochures.

Monterey

Working-class Monterey is all about the sea. What draws many visitors is a world-class aquarium overlooking Monterey Bay National Marine Sanctuary, which protects dense kelp forests and a sublime variety of marine life, including seals and sea lions, dolphins and whales. The city itself possesses the best-preserved historical evidence of California's Spanish and Mexican periods, with many restored adobe buildings. An afternoon's wander through downtown's historic quarter promises to be more edifying than time spent in the tourist ghettos of Fisherman's Wharf and Cannery Row.

◉ Sights

Monterey Bay Aquarium Aquarium
See p24.

Cannery Row Historic Site

(🖘) John Steinbeck's novel *Cannery Row* immortalized the sardine-canning business that was Monterey's lifeblood for the first half of the 20th century. A bronze bust of the Pulitzer Prize–winning writer sits at the bottom of Prescott Ave, just steps from the unabashedly touristy experience that the famous row has devolved into. The historical Cannery Workers Shacks at the base of flowery Bruce Ariss Way provide a sobering reminder of the hard lives led by Filipino, Japanese, Spanish and other immigrant laborers.

★ Monterey State Historic Park Historic Site

(☑ audio tour 831-998-9458, info 831-649-7118; www.parks.ca.gov) 🌠 FREE Old Monterey is home to an extraordinary assemblage of 19th-century brick and adobe buildings, administered as Monterey State Historic Park, all found along a 2-mile self-guided walking tour portentously called the 'Path of History.' You can inspect dozens of buildings, many with charming gardens; expect some to be open while others aren't, according to a capricious schedule dictated by unfortunate state-park budget cutbacks.

🏃 Activities

Cycling & Mountain Biking

Along an old railway line, the Monterey Peninsula Recreational Trail travels for 18 car-free miles along the waterfront, passing Cannery Row en route to Lovers Point in Pacific Grove. Road-cycling enthusiasts can make the round trip to Carmel along the 17-Mile Drive. Mountain bikers head to Fort Ord National Monument to pedal more than 80 miles of single-track and fire roads; the Sea Otter Classic (www.seaotterclassic.com) races there in mid-April.

Adventures by the Sea Cycling, Kayaking

(☑ 831-372-1807; www.adventuresbythesea.com; 299 Cannery Row; rental per day kayak or bicycle $30, SUP set $50, tours from $60; 🖘) Beach cruisers, electric bike and water-sports gear rentals and tours available at multiple locations on Cannery Row and downtown (☑ 831-372-1807; www.adventuresbythesea.com; 210 Alvarado St; 🖘).

Whale-Watching

You can spot whales off the coast of Monterey Bay year-round. The season for blue and humpback whales runs from April to early December, while gray whales pass by from mid-December through March. Tour boats depart from Fisherman's Wharf and Moss Landing. Reserve trips at least a day in advance; be prepared for a bumpy, cold ride.

Monterey Whale Watching Boat Tour

(☑ 831-205-2370, 888-223-9153; www.montereywhalewatching.com; 96 Fisherman's Wharf; 2½hr tour adult/child 5-11yr $45/35; 🖘) Several daily departures; no children under age five or pregnant women allowed.

Monterey Bay Whale Watch Boat Tour

(☑ 831-375-4658; www.montereybaywhalewatch.com; 84 Fisherman's Wharf; 3hr tour adult/child 4-12yr from $40/27; 🖘) Morning and afternoon departures; young children are welcome on board.

Monterey

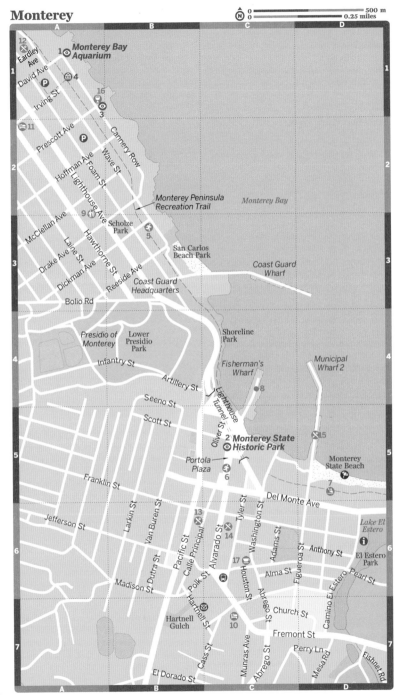

Monterey

Diving & Snorkeling

Monterey Bay offers world-renowned diving and snorkeling, including off Lovers Point in Pacific Grove and at Point Lobos State Natural Reserve south of Carmel-by-the-Sea. You'll want a wetsuit year-round. In summer upwelling currents carry cold water from the deep canyon below the bay, sending a rich supply of nutrients up toward the surface level to feed the bay's diverse marine life. These frigid currents also account for the bay's chilly water temperatures and the summer fog that blankets the peninsula.

Kayaking & Surfing

Monterey Bay Kayaks   Kayaking

(⌨ 831-373-5357, 800-649-5357; www. montereybaykayaks.com; 693 Del Monte Ave; kayak or SUP set rental per day from $30, tours from $55) Rents kayaks and SUP equipment, offers paddling lessons and leads guided tours of Monterey Bay, including full-moon and sunrise trips.

Sunshine Freestyle Surf & Sport   Surfing

(⌨ 831-375-5015; www.sunshinefreestyle.com; 443 Lighthouse Ave; rental surfboard/wetsuit/boogie board from $20/10/7) Monterey's oldest surf shop rents and sells all the surfing gear you'll need. Staff grudgingly dole out local tips.

◎ Sleeping

Book ahead for special events, on weekends and in summer. To avoid the tourist congestion and jacked-up prices of Cannery Row, look to Pacific Grove. Cheaper motels line Munras Ave, south of downtown, and N Fremont St, east of Hwy 1.

HI Monterey Hostel   Hostel $

(⌨ 831-649-0375; www.montereyhostel.org; 778 Hawthorne St; dm with shared bath $26-35; ⊙ check-in 4-10pm; @🛜) Four blocks from Cannery Row and the aquarium, this simple, clean hostel houses single-sex and mixed dorms, as well as private rooms (call for rates). Budget backpackers stuff themselves silly with make-your-own pancake breakfasts. Reservations strongly recommended. Take MST bus 1 from downtown's Transit Plaza.

Veterans Memorial Park Campground   Campground $

(⌨ 831-646-3865; www.monterey.org; tent & RV sites $27) Tucked into the forest, this municipal campground has 40 grassy, nonreservable sites near a nature preserve's hiking trails. Amenities include coin-op hot showers, flush toilets, drinking water and barbecue fire pits. Three-night maximum stay.

Casa Munras   Boutique Hotel $$

(⌨ 800-222-2446, 831-375-2411; www. hotelcasamunras.com; 700 Munras Ave; r from $120; @🛜⚟🐾) Built around an adobe hacienda once owned by a 19th-century Spanish colonial don, chic modern rooms come with lofty beds and some gas fireplaces, all inside two-story motel-esque buildings. Splash in a heated outdoor pool, unwind at the tapas bar or take a sea-salt scrub in the tiny spa. Pet fee $50.

◎ Eating & Drinking

Uphill from Cannery Row, Lighthouse Ave is chock-a-block with casual, budget-friendly eateries, from Hawaiian barbecue to Middle Eastern kebabs. Prowl downtown's Alvarado St, touristy Cannery Row and locals-only Lighthouse Ave for more watering holes.

Old Monterey Marketplace
Market $

(www.oldmonterey.org; Alvarado St, btwn Del Monte Ave & Pearl St; ⊘4-7pm Tue Sep-May, to 8pm Jun-Aug; 👪) 🍴 Rain or shine, head downtown on Tuesdays for farm-fresh fruit and veggies, artisan cheeses, international food stalls and a scrumptious 'baker's alley.'

First Awakenings
American $$

(www.firstawakenings.net; American Tin Cannery, 125 Oceanview Blvd; mains $8-12; ⊘7am-2pm Mon-Fri, to 2:30pm Sat & Sun; 👪) Sweet and savory, all-American breakfasts and lunches and bottomless pitchers of coffee merrily weigh down outdoor tables at this cafe uphill from the aquarium. Try the unusual 'bluegerm' pancakes or a spicy Sonoran frittata.

Montrio Bistro
Californian $$$

(☎831-648-8880; www.montrio.com; 414 Calle Principal; mains $17-29; ⊘5-10pm Sun-Thu, to 11pm Fri & Sat; 👪) Inside a 1910 firehouse, Montrio looks dolled up with leather walls and iron trellises, but the tables have butcher paper and crayons for kids. The eclectic seasonal menu mixes local, organic fare with Californian, Asian and European flair, including tapas-style small bites and mini desserts.

🍷 Drinking & Nightlife

Prowl downtown's Alvarado St, touristy Cannery Row and locals-only Lighthouse Ave for more watering holes.

A Taste of Monterey
Wine Bar

(www.atasteofmonterey.com; 700 Cannery Row; tasting fee $10-20; ⊘11am-7pm Sun-Wed, to 8pm Thu-Sat) Sample medal-winning Monterey County wines from as far away as the Santa Lucia Highlands while soaking up dreamy sea views, then peruse thoughtful exhibits on barrel-making and cork production.

East Village Coffee Lounge
Cafe, Lounge

(www.eastvillagecoffeelounge.com; 498 Washington St; ⊘6am-late Mon-Fri, from 7am Sat & Sun; 🛜) Downtown coffee shop on a busy corner brews with fair-trade, organic beans. At night, it pulls off a big-city lounge vibe with film, open-mic and live-music nights and an all-important booze license.

Information

Monterey Visitors Center (☎877-666-8373, 831-657-6400; www.seemonterey.com; 401 Camino El Estero; ⊘9am-6pm Mon-Sat, to 5pm Sun, closing 1hr earlier Nov-Mar) Free tourist brochures; ask for a *Monterey County Literary & Film Map*.

San Luis Obispo

Almost midway between LA and San Francisco, at the junction of Hwys 101 and 1, San Luis Obispo is a popular overnight stop for road trippers. With no must-see attractions, SLO might not seem to warrant much of your time. Even so, this low-key town has an enviably high quality of life – in fact, it has been named America's happiest city. CalPoly university students inject a healthy dose of hubbub into the city's streets, bars and cafes throughout the school year. Nestled at the base of the Santa Lucia foothills, SLO is just a grape's throw from Edna Valley wineries too.

◉ Sights & Activities

San Luis Obispo Creek, once used to irrigate mission orchards, flows through downtown. Uphill from Higuera St, Mission Plaza is a shady oasis with restored adobe buildings and fountains overlooking the creek. Look for the Moon Tree, a coast redwood grown from a seed that journeyed on board Apollo 14's lunar mission. For more hiking with ocean views, head to Montaña de Oro State Park, not far away.

Bishop Peak
Hiking

SLO's most popular hike summits Bishop Peak (1546ft), the tallest of the Nine Sisters, a chain of volcanic peaks that stretches north to Morro Bay. The 2.2-mile one-way trail starts in a grove of live oaks (watch out for poison oak) and heads uphill along rocky, mostly exposed switchbacks. Carefully scramble up boulders at the tippy-top for panoramic views.

🛏 Sleeping

Motels cluster off Hwy 101, especially off Monterey St northeast of downtown and around Santa Rosa St (Hwy 1).

HI Hostel Obispo
Hostel $

(☎805-544-4678; www.hostelobispo.com; 1617 Santa Rosa St; dm $27-31, r from $60, all with shared bath; ⊘check-in 4:30-10pm; @🛜) 🍴 On a tree-lined street near the train station, this solar-empowered, avocado-colored hostel inhabits a converted Victorian, which gives it a bit of a B&B feel. Amenities include a kitchen, bike rentals (from $10 per day) and complimentary sourdough pancakes and coffee for breakfast. BYOT (bring your own towel).

Peach Tree Inn
Motel **$$**

(☑ 800-227-6396, 805-543-3170; www.peachtreeinn.com; 2001 Monterey St; ☉ office 7am-11pm; @ 🛜) The folksy, nothing-fancy motel rooms here are inviting, especially those right by the creek or with rocking chairs on wooden porches overlooking grassy lawns, eucalyptus trees and rose gardens. Continental breakfast features homemade breads.

San Luis Creek Lodge
Hotel **$$$**

(☑ 800-593-0333, 805-541-1122; www.sanluiscreeklodge.com; 1941 Monterey St; r incl breakfast $149-269; ✳ @ 🛜) Rubbing shoulders with neighboring motels, this boutique inn has fresh, spacious rooms with divine beds (and some have gas fireplaces and jetted tubs) inside three whimsically mismatched buildings built in Tudor, California arts-and-crafts and Southern plantation styles. DVDs, chess sets and board games are free to borrow.

Humpback whale, Monterey
TORY KALLMAN / GETTY IMAGES ©

✖ Eating

★ San Luis Obispo Farmers Market
Market **$**

(www.downtownslo.com; ☉ 6-9pm Thu) The county's biggest and best weekly farmers market turns downtown SLO's Higuera St into a giant street party, with smokin' barbecues, overflowing fruit and veggie stands, live music and free sidewalk entertainment, from salvation peddlers to wackadoodle political activists. Rain cancels it.

Meze Wine Bar & Bistro
Mediterranean **$$**

(www.mezewinebar.com; 1880 Santa Barbara Ave; mains $10-20; ☉ 11am-9pm Mon-Wed, to 10pm Thu-Sat) Hidden downhill from the Amtrak station, this tiny wine shop, gourmet market and tapas-style bar is an eclectic gem. Gather with friends around the cheese and charcuterie board, or stop in for a hand-crafted sandwich with a quinoa salad.

★ Luna Red
Fusion **$$$**

(☑ 805-540-5243; www.lunaredslo.com; 1023 Chorro St; shared plates $6-20, mains $20-39; ☉ 11am-9pm Mon-Wed, to 11:30pm Thu-Fri, 9:30am-11:30pm Sat, to 9pm Sun; 🍴) 🌱 Local bounty from the land and sea, artisan cheeses and farmers-market produce pervade the chef's Californian, Asian and Mediterranean

small-plates menu. Cocktails and glowing lanterns enhance a sophisticated ambience indoors, or linger over brunch on the mission-view garden patio. Reservations recommended.

🍸 Drinking & Nightlife

Downtown, Higuera St is littered with college-student-jammed bars.

Downtown Brewing Co
Brewery

(☑ 805-543-1843; www.slobrew.com; 1119 Garden St) Nicknamed SLO Brew, this study in rafters and exposed brick has plenty of craft beers to go, along with filling pub grub. Downstairs, you'll find DJs or live bands (including some surprisingly famous acts) on many nights.

Kreuzberg
Cafe

(www.kreuzbergcalifornia.com; 685 Higuera St; ☉ 7:30am-10pm; 🛜) Shabby-chic coffeehouse and roaster has earned a fervent following with its comfy couches, sprawling bookshelves, local art and occasional live music.

Information

SLO's compact downtown is bisected by the parallel one-way arteries Higuera St and Marsh St. Banks with 24-hour ATMs are off Marsh St, near the post office.

San Luis Obispo Visitor Center (☑ 805-781-2777; www.visitslo.com; 895 Monterey St; ☉ 10am-5pm Sun-Wed, to 7pm Thu-Sat) Free maps and tourist brochures.

Santa Barbara County

Chic Santa Barbara's red-tiled roofs, white stucco buildings and Mediterranean vibe give credence to its claim of being the 'American Riviera.'

Santa Barbara

👁 Sights

★ Mission Santa Barbara *Church*

(www.santabarbaramission.org; 2201 Laguna St; adult/child 5-15yr $6/1; ⊙ 9am-4:30pm Apr-Oct, to 4:15pm Nov-Mar; **P**) California's 'Queen of the Missions' reigns above the city on a hilltop perch over a mile northwest of downtown. Its imposing Doric facade, an architectural homage to an ancient Roman chapel, is topped by an unusual twin bell tower. Inside the mission's 1820 stone church, notice the striking Chumash artwork. Outside is an eerie cemetery – skull carvings hang over the door leading outside – with 4000 Chumash graves and the elaborate mausoleums of early California settlers.

Santa Barbara County Courthouse *Historic Site*

See p21.

Stearns Wharf *Historic Site*

(www.stearnswharf.org; **P**) **FREE** The southern end of State St gives way onto Stearns Wharf, a rough wooden pier lined with souvenir shops, snack stands and seafood shacks. Built in 1872, it's the oldest continuously operating wharf on the West Coast, although the actual structure has been rebuilt more than once. During the 1940s it was co-owned by tough-guy actor Jimmy Cagney and his brothers. If you've got kids, tow them inside the Ty Warner Sea Center.

Parking on the wharf costs $2.50 per hour; the first 90 minutes are free with merchant validation. But trust us, you'd rather walk than drive over the wharf's bumpy wooden slats. The wharf entrance is a stop on MTD's downtown and waterfront shuttles.

Santa Barbara Museum of Art *Museum*

(☎ 805-963-4364; www.sbma.net; 1130 State St; adult/child 6-17yr $10/6, all free 5-8pm Thu; ⊙ 11am-5pm Tue-Wed & Fri-Sun, to 8pm Thu) This thoughtfully curated, bite-sized art museum displays European and American masters – think Matisse and Diego Rivera – along with contemporary photography, classical antiquities and though-provoking temporary exhibits. Traipse up to the 2nd floor, where impressive Asian art collections include an intricate, colorful Tibetan sand mandala and the iron-and-leather armor of a Japanese warrior. Guided tours usually start at 1pm daily. There's also an interactive children's space, a museum shop and a cafe.

🏃 Activities

Cycling

A paved recreational path stretches 3 miles along the waterfront in both directions from

Stearns Wharf, west to Leadbetter Beach beyond the harbor and east just past East Beach. For more pedaling routes, Bike Santa Barbara County (www.bike-santabarbara.org) offers free downloadable DIY cycling tours of the city, mountains and Wine Country, along with links to bicycle rentals and specialty shops.

Kayaking

Paddle the calm waters of Santa Barbara's harbor or the coves of the Gaviota coast, or hitch a ride to the Channel Islands for awesome sea caves.

Boating & Whale-Watching

Some tour companies offer year-round whale-watching boat trips, mostly to see grays in winter and spring, and humpbacks and blues in summer.

Surfing

Unless you're a novice, conditions are too mellow in summer – come back in winter when ocean swells kick back up. Santa Barbara's Leadbetter Point is best for beginners. Experts-only Rincon Point awaits just outside Carpinteria.

Hiking

Gorgeous day hikes await in the foothills of the Santa Ynez Mountains and elsewhere in the Los Padres National Forest. Most trails cut through rugged chaparral and steep canyons – sweat it out and savor jaw-dropping coastal views. Spring and fall are the best seasons for hiking, when temperatures are moderate. Always carry plenty of extra water and watch out for poison oak.

To find even more local trails to explore, browse Santa Barbara Hikes (www.santabarbarahikes.com) online or visit the Los Padres National Forest Headquarters (☎805-968-6640; www.fs.usda.gov/lpnf; 6755 Hollister Ave, Goleta; ⊙8:30am-noon & 1-4:30pm Mon-Fri), west of the airport (from Hwy 101, exit Glen Annie Rd southbound onto Storke Rd).

🛏 Sleeping

Prepare for sticker shock: basic motel rooms by the beach command over $200 in summer. Don't show up at the last minute without reservations and expect to find any reasonably priced rooms, especially not on weekends. Cheaper motels cluster along upper State St and Hwy 101 northbound to Goleta and southbound to Carpinteria, Ventura and Camarillo.

★ Santa Barbara
Auto Camp   Campground $$

(☎888-405-7553; http://autocamp.com/sb; 2717 De La Vina St; d $175-215; P❂❄🛜🚗🐾) 🍴 Bed down with vintage style in one of five shiny metal Airstream trailers parked near upper State St, north of downtown. All five architect-designed trailers have unique perks, such as a clawfoot tub or extra twin-size beds for kiddos, as well as a full kitchen and complimentary cruiser bikes to borrow. Book ahead; two-night minimum may apply. Pet fee $25.

Hotel Indigo   Boutique Hotel $$

(☎805-966-6586, 877-270-1392; www.indigosantabarbara.com; 121 State St; r from $170; P❂@🛜🐾) 🍴 Poised between downtown and the beach, this petite Euro-chic boutique hotel has all the right touches: curated contemporary-art displays, rooftop patios and ecofriendly green-design elements like a living-plant wall. Peruse local-interest and art history books in the library nook, or retreat to your room and wrap yourself up in a plush bathrobe. Parking $14.

Agave Inn   Motel $$

(☎805-687-6009; http://agaveinnsb.com; 3222 State St; r incl breakfast from $119; P❂🛜) While it's still just a motel at heart, this boutique-on-a-budget property's 'Mexican pop meets modern' motif livens things up with a color palette from a Frieda Kahlo painting. Flat-screen TVs, microwaves, minifridges and air-con make it a standout option. Family-sized rooms have kitchenettes and pull-out sofa beds. Continental breakfast included.

★ El Encanto   Luxury Hotel $$$

(☎805-845-5800, 800-393-5315; www.elencanto.com; 800 Alvarado Pl; d from $475; P❂@🛜🏊🚗🐾) Triumphantly reborn, this 1920s icon of Santa Barbara style is a hilltop hideaway for travelers who demand the very best of everything. An infinity pool gazes out at the Pacific, while flower-filled gardens, fireplace lounges, a full-service spa and private bungalows with sun-drenched patios concoct the glamorous atmosphere perfectly fitted to SoCal socialites. Grab sunset drinks on the ocean-view terrace. Parking $35.

🍴 Eating

Restaurants abound along downtown's State St and by the waterfront, where you'll find a few gems among the touristy claptrap. More

Downtown Santa Barbara

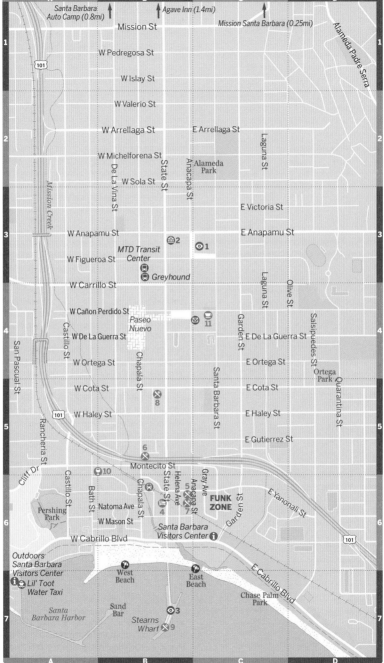

Downtown Santa Barbara

⊙ Sights

🛏 Sleeping

✖ Eating

☕ Drinking & Nightlife

creative kitchens are found down in the Funk Zone. East of downtown, Milpas St is lined with Mexicali taco shops.

Lucky Penny   Pizzeria $

(www.luckypennysb.com; 127 Anacapa St; mains $7-10, pizzas $10-15; ☺7am-9pm Mon-Sat, from 9am Sun; ✍) With shiny exterior walls covered in copper pennies, this pizzeria next to Lark restaurant is always jam-packed. It's worth the wait for a crispy pizza topped with smoked mozzarella and pork-and-fennel sausage or a wood-oven-fired lamb meatball sandwich. Turn up before 11am for crazily inventive breakfast pizzas and farm-fresh egg skillets.

Lilly's Taquería   Mexican $

(http://lillystacos.com; 310 Chapala St; items from $1.60; ☺10:30am-9pm Sun-Mon & Wed-Thu, to 10pm Fri & Sat) There's almost always a line roping around this downtown taco shack at lunchtime. But it goes fast, so you'd best be snappy with your order – the *adobada* (marinated pork) and *lengua* (beef tongue) are stand-out choices. Second location in Goleta west of the airport, off Hwy 101.

**★ Santa Barbara
Shellfish Company**   Seafood $$

(www.sbfishhouse.com; 230 Stearns Wharf; dishes $4-19; ☺11am-9pm; P♿) 'From sea to skillet to plate' sums up this end-of-the-wharf sea-

food shack that's more of a buzzing counter joint than a sit-down restaurant. Chase away the seagulls as you chow down on garlic-baked clams, crab cakes and coconut-fried shrimp at wooden picnic tables outside. Awesome lobster bisque, ocean views and the same location for over 25 years.

Olio Pizzeria   Italian $$

(✆805-899-2699; www.oliopizzeria.com; 11 W Victoria St; shared plates $7-24, lunch mains $9-17; ☺usually 11:30am-10pm) Just around the corner from State St, this high-ceilinged pizzeria with a happening wine bar proffers crispy, wood oven-baked pizzas, platters of imported cheeses and meats, garden-fresh *insalate* (salads), savory traditional Italian antipasti and sweet *dolci* (desserts). The entrance is off the parking lot alleyway.

★ Lark   Californian $$$

(✆805-284-0370; www.thelarksb.com; 131 Anacapa St; shared plates $5-32, mains $24-38; ☺5-10pm Tue-Sun, bar till midnight) ✍ There's no better place in Santa Barbara County to taste the bountiful farm and fishing goodness of this stretch of SoCal coast. Named after an antique Pullman railway car, this chef-run restaurant in the Funk Zone morphs its menu with the seasons, presenting unique flavor combinations like fried olives with chorizo aioli and chile-spiced mussels in lemongrass-lime broth. Make reservations.

🍷 Drinking & Nightlife

On lower State St, most of the meat-market watering holes have happy hours, tiny dance floors and rowdy college nights. Just south of Hwy 101, the arty Funk Zone's eclectic mix of bars and wine-tasting rooms is a trendy scene.

★ Figueroa Mountain Brewing Co   Bar

(www.figmtnbrew.com; 137 Anacapa St; ☺11am-11pm) Father and son brewers have brought their gold medal-winning hoppy IPA, Danish red lager, and double IPA from Santa Barbara's Wine Country to the Funk Zone. Clink pint glasses on the taproom's open-air patio while acoustic acts play. Enter on Yanonali St.

Handlebar Coffee Roasters   Cafe

(www.handlebarcoffee.com; 128 E Cañon Perdido St; ☺7am-5pm Mon-Sat, from 8am Sun; ♿) Bicycle-themed coffee shop brews rich coffee and espresso drinks from small-batch roasted beans. Sit and sip yours on the sunny patio.

Brewhouse
Brewery

(sbbrewhouse.com; 229 W Montecito St; ⊙11am-11pm Sun-Thu, to midnight Fri & Sat; 🐀🌟) Down by the railroad tracks, the boisterous Brewhouse crafts its own unique small-batch beer (Saint Barb's Belgian-style ales rule), serves wines by the glass and has cool art and rockin' live music Wednesday to Saturday nights.

- -
☆ Entertainment

Santa Barbara's appreciation of the arts is evidenced not only by the variety of performances available on any given night, but also its gorgeous, often historic venues. For a current calender of live music and special events, check www.independent.com online or pick up Friday's *Scene* guide in the *Santa Barbara News-Press*.

ℹ Information

Santa Barbara Visitors Center (✑ 805-568-1811, 805-965-3021; www.santabarbaraca.com; 1 Garden St; ⊙ 9am-5pm Mon-Sat & 10am-5pm Sun Feb-Oct; 9am-4pm Mon-Sat Nov-Jan) Pick up maps and brochures while consulting with the helpful but busy staff. The website offers free downloadable DIY touring maps and itineraries, from famous movie locations to wine trails, art galleries and outdoors fun. Self-pay metered parking lot nearby.

Santa Barbara Wine Country

Oak-dotted hillsides, winding country lanes, rows of sweetly heavy grapevines stretching as far as the eye can see – it's hard not to gush about the Santa Ynez and Santa Maria Valleys and the Santa Rita Hills wine regions. From fancy convertibles and Harleys to ecofriendly touring vans and road bikes, you'll find an eclectic, friendly mix of travelers sharing these bucolic back roads.

The big-name appellations for Santa Barbara's Wine Country are the Santa Ynez Valley, Santa Maria Valley and Santa Rita Hills, plus smaller Happy Canyon and upstart Ballard Canyon. Wine-tasting rooms abound in Los Olivos and Solvang, handy for anyone with limited time.

The Santa Ynez Valley, where you'll find most of the wineries, lies south of the Santa Maria Valley. Hwy 246 runs east–west, via Solvang, across the bottom of the Santa Ynez Valley, connecting Hwy 101 with Hwy 154. North–south secondary roads bordered by

vineyards include Alamo Pintado Rd from Hwy 246 to Los Olivos, and Refugio Rd between Santa Ynez and Ballard.

A half-day trip will allow you to see one winery or tasting room, have lunch and return to Santa Barbara. Otherwise make it a full day and plan to have lunch and possibly dinner before returning to the city.

Foxen Canyon Wine Trail

The scenic Foxen Canyon Wine Trail (www.foxencanyonwinetrail.com) runs north from Hwy 154, just west of Los Olivos, deep into the heart of the rural Santa Maria Valley. It's a must-see for oenophiles or anyone wanting to get off the beaten path. For the most part, it follows Foxen Canyon Rd.

★ Foxen
Winery

(✑805-937-4251; www.foxenvineyard.com; 7200 & 7600 Foxen Canyon Rd, Santa Maria; tastings $10; ⊙11am-4pm) On what was once a working cattle ranch, Foxen crafts warm Syrah, steel-cut Chardonnay, full-fruited pinot noir and rich Rhône-style wines, all sourced from standout vineyards. The newer tasting room is solar-powered, while the old 'shack' – a dressed-down space with a corrugated-metal roof, funky-cool decor and leafy patio – pours Bordeaux-style and Cal-Ital varietals under the 'Foxen 7200' label.

Demetria Estate
Winery

(✑805-686-2345; www.demetriaestate.com; 6701 Foxen Canyon Rd, Los Olivos; tastings $20; ⊙by appt only) ✆ This hilltop retreat has the curving arches and thick wooden doors of your hospitable Greek uncle's country house, with epic views of vineyards and rolling hillsides. Tastings are by appointment only, but worth it just to sample the biodynamically farmed Chardonnay, Syrah and viognier, plus rave-worthy Rhône-style red blends.

Zaca Mesa Winery
Winery

(www.zacamesa.com; 6905 Foxen Canyon Rd, Los Olivos; tastings $10; ⊙10am-4pm daily year-round, to 5pm Fri & Sat late May–early Sep) Stop by this barn-style tasting room for a rustic, sipping-on-the-farm ambience. Santa Barbara's highest-elevation winery, Zaca Mesa is known not only for its estate-grown Rhône varietals and signature Z Cuvée red blend and Z Blanc white blend, but also a life-sized outdoor chessboard, a tree-shaded picnic area that's dog-friendly and a short, scenic trail overlooking the vineyards.

Santa Rita Hills Wine Trail

When it comes to country-road scenery, eco-conscious farming practices and top-notch pinot noir, the less-traveled Santa Rita Hills (www.staritahills.com) region holds its own. Almost a dozen tasting rooms line an easy driving loop west of Hwy 101 via Santa Rosa Rd and Hwy 246. Be prepared to share the roads with cyclists and an occasional John Deere tractor. More artisan winemarkers hide out in the industrial warehouses of Buellton near Hwy 101 and farther afield in Lompoc's 'Wine Ghetto' (www.lompoctrail.com).

Alma Rosa Winery & Vineyards   Winery

(📞 805-688-9090;   www.almarosawinery.com; tastings $5-15;   ⊙ 11am-4:30pm) 🍷 Richard Sanford left the powerhouse winery bearing his name to start this new winery with his wife, Thekla, using sustainable, organic farming techniques. Cacti and cobblestones welcome you to the ranch, reached via a long, winding gravel driveway. Vineyard-designated pinot noir and fine pinot blanc and pinot gris are what's poured. Call ahead for directions to the new tasting room.

Wine-tasting, Santa Barbara
BRENT WINEBRENNER / GETTY IMAGES ©

and stingy pours often disappoint, but thankfully that's not the case at better wine-tasting rooms.

Sanford Winery   Winery

(www.sanfordwinery.com; 5010 Santa Rosa Rd, Lompoc; tastings $15-20, incl tour $25; ⊙ 11am-4pm Sun-Thu, to 5pm Fri & Sat Mar-Oct, 11am-4pm daily Nov-Feb) Be enchanted by this romantic tasting room built of stone and handmade adobe bricks, all embraced by estate vineyards on the historic Rancho La Rinconda property. Watch the sun sink over the vineyards from the back patio with a glass of silky pinot noir or citrusy Chardonnay in hand. Winery tours are typically given at 11:30am daily (no reservations).

Babcock   Winery

(www.babcockwinery.com; 5175 E Hwy 146, Lompoc; tastings $12-15; ⊙ 10:30am-5pm) Family-owned vineyards overflow with different grape varietals – Chardonnay, Sauvignon Blanc, Pinot Gris, Pinot Noir, Syrah, Cabernet Sauvignon, Merlot and more – that let innovative small-lot winemaker Bryan Babcock be the star. 'Slice of Heaven' pinot noir alone is worthy of a pilgrimage to this eclectically furnished tasting room with elevated views.

Santa Ynez Valley

Popular wineries cluster between Los Olivos and Solvang along Alamo Pintado Rd and Refugio Rd, south of Roblar Ave and west of Hwy 154. Noisy tour groups, harried staff

Beckmen Vineyards   Winery

(www.beckmenvineyards.com; 2670 Ontiveros Rd, Solvang; tastings $10-15; ⊙ 11am-5pm) 🍷 Bring a picnic to the pondside gazebo at this tranquil winery, where estate-grown Rhône varieties flourish on the unique terroir of Purisima Mountain. Using biodynamic farming principles, natural (not chemical), means are used to prevent pests. To sample superb Syrah and a rare cuvée blend with grenache, Mourvèdre and Counoise, follow Roblar Ave west of Hwy 154 to Ontiveros Rd.

Lincourt Vineyard   Winery

(www.lincourtwines.com; 1711 Alamo Pintado Rd, Solvang; tastings from $10; ⊙ 10am-5pm) Respected winemaker Bill Foley, who runs Firestone Vineyard on the Foxen Canyon Wine Trail, founded this vineyard first in the late 1990s on a former dairy farm. You can still see the original 1926 farmhouse built from a Sears catalog kit. Inside the cottage's tasting room, sip finely crafted Syrah, pinot noir and a dry French-style rosé, all made from grapes grown in the Santa Maria Valley and Santa Rita Hills.

Kalyra Winery   Winery

(www.kalyrawinery.com; 343 N Refugio Rd, Santa Ynez; tastings $10-12; ⊙ 11am-5pm Mon-Fri, from 10am Sat & Sun) Australian Mike Brown has traveled halfway around the world to combine his

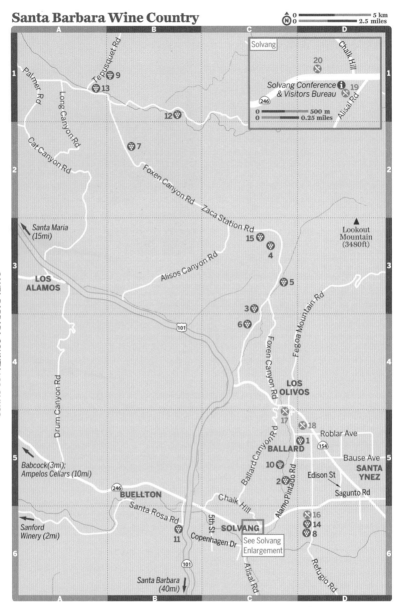

two loves: surfing and winemaking. Try one of his full-bodied red blends, unusual white varietals or sweet dessert wines (the orange muscat is a crowd-pleaser), all in bottles with Aboriginal art-inspired labels. Kalyra also pours at a smaller tasting room on Santa Barbara's Urban Wine Trail.

Los Olivos

POP 1130

The posh ranching town of Los Olivos is many visitors' first stop when exploring Santa Barbara's Wine Country. Its four-block-long main street is lined with rustic wine-tasting

Santa Barbara Wine Country

◎ Sights

rooms, bistros and boutiques seemingly airlifted straight out of Napa.

✗ Eating

Los Olivos Grocery   Market, Deli $

(http://losolivosgrocery.com; 2621 W Hwy 154, Santa Ynez; ⊗7am-9pm) This tiny local market heaps barbecue tri-tip sandwiches, artisan breads, specialty cheeses and everything you'll need for a vineyard picnic, or grab a table on the front porch.

Los Olivos Café & Wine
Merchant   Californian, Mediterranean $$$

(☑805-688-7265; www.losolivoscafe.com; 2879 Grand Ave; mains breakfast $9-12, lunch & dinner $12-29; ⊗11:30am-8:30pm daily, also 8-10:30am Sat & Sun) With white canopies and a wisteria-covered trellis, this wine-country landmark (as seen in *Sideways*) swirls up a casual-chic SoCal ambience. It stays open between lunch and dinner for antipasto platters, hearty salads and crispy pizzas and wine flights at the bar.

Solvang

POP 5345

This Santa Ynez Valley town holds tight to its Danish heritage, or at least stereo-

typical images thereof. With its knick-knack stores and cutesy motels, the town is almost as sticky-sweet as the Scandinavian pastries foisted upon the wandering crowds of day trippers. Solvang's kitschy charms make it worth visiting if only to gawk.

✗ Eating

El Rancho Market   Supermarket $

(http://elranchomarket.com; 2886 Mission Dr; ⊗6am-11pm) East of downtown, this upscale supermarket – with a full deli, smokin' barbecued meats and an espresso bar – is the best place to fill your picnic basket before heading out to the wineries.

Solvang Restaurant   Bakery $

(www.solvangrestaurant.com; 1672 Copenhagen Dr; items from $4; ⊗6am-3pm or 4pm Mon-Fri, to 5pm Sat & Sun; ☖) Duck around the Danish-inscribed beams with decorative borders to order *ableskivers* – round pancake popovers covered in powdered sugar and raspberry jam. They're so popular, there's even a special take-out window.

★ Succulent Café   Californian $$

(☑805-691-9235; www.succulentcafe.com; 1555 Mission Dr; mains breakfast & lunch $9-13, dinner $19-29; ⊗breakfast 8:30am-noon Sat & Sun; lunch 11am-3pm Mon & Wed-Fri, to 4pm Sat & Sun; dinner 5:30-9pm Mon & Wed-Sun) ✎ An inspired menu allows farm-fresh ingredients to speak for themselves at this family-owned gourmet cafe and market. Fuel up on breakfast biscuits stuffed with cinnamon-cumin pork tenderloin and pineapple chutney with bacon gravy, buttermilk-fried chicken salad and artisan grilled-cheese sandwiches for lunch, or pumpkin seed-crusted lamb for dinner. On sunny days, eat outside on the patio.

❶ Information

Solvang is the busiest hub for wine-country visitors.

Solvang Conference & Visitors Bureau
(☑805-688-6144, 800-468-6765; www.solvangusa.com; 1639 Copenhagen Dr, Solvang; ⊗9am-5pm) Pick up free tourist brochures and winery maps at this kiosk in the town center, by the municipal parking lot and public restrooms.

Los Angeles

LA is a beacon for countless small-town dreamers, rockers and risk-takers, an open-minded angel who encourages her people to live and let live without judgment or shame.

👁 Sights & Activities

Hollywood & Around

Hollywood Walk of Fame   Landmark

(www.walkoffame.com; Hollywood Blvd) Big Bird, Bob Hope, Marilyn Monroe and Aretha Franklin are among the stars being sought out, worshipped, photographed and stepped on along the Hollywood Walk of Fame. Since 1960 more than 2400 performers – from legends to bit-part players – have been honored with a pink-marble sidewalk star.

Grauman's Chinese Theatre   Landmark

(☎ 323-463-9576;   www.tclchinesetheatres.com; 6925 Hollywood Blvd; tours & movie tickets adult/child/senior $13.50/6.50/11.50) Ever wondered what it's like to be in George Clooney's shoes? Just find his footprints in the forecourt of this world-famous movie palace. The exotic pagoda theater – complete with temple bells and stone heaven dogs from China – has shown movies since 1927 when Cecil B DeMille's *The King of Kings* first flickered across the screen.

Hollywood Sign   Landmark

LA's most famous landmark first appeared in the hills in 1923 as an advertising gimmick for a real-estate development called 'Hollywoodland'. Each letter is 50ft tall and made of sheet metal. Once aglow with 4000 light bulbs, the sign even had its own caretaker who lived behind the 'L' until 1939.

Hollywood Bowl   Landmark

(www.hollywoodbowl.com;   2301 Highland Ave; rehearsals free, performance costs vary; ⊘ Apr-Sep; P) Summers in LA wouldn't be the same without this chill spot for symphonies under the stars, and big-name acts from Baaba Maal and Sigur Rós to Radiohead and Paul McCartney. A huge natural amphitheater, the Hollywood Bowl has been around since 1922 and has great sound.

Griffith Park   Park

(☎ 323-913-4688;   www.laparks.org/dos/parks/griffithpk; 4730 Crystal Springs Dr; ⊘ 5am-10:30pm, trails sunrise-sunset; P) FREE A gift to the city in 1896 by mining mogul Griffith J Griffith, and five times the size of New York's Central Park, Griffith Park is one of the country's largest urban green spaces. There you'll find a major outdoor theater, the city zoo, two museums, golf courses, playgrounds, 53 miles of hiking trails, Batman's caves and the Hollywood sign. It's crowned by the iconic 1935 Observatory (☎ 213-473-0800;   www.griffithobservatory.org; 2800 E Observatory Rd; admission free, planetarium shows adult/child $7/3; ⊘ noon-10pm Tue-Fri, from 10am Sat & Sun; P) FREE, a first-class planetarium and wonderful Instagram photo-op. Don't miss it.

Farmers Market & Around   Market

(www.farmersmarketla.com; 6333 W 3rd St, Fairfax District; ☺9am-9pm Mon-Fri, to 8pm Sat, 10am-7pm Sun; Ⓟ🅗) **FREE** Long before the city was flooded with farmers markets, there was the Farmers Market. From fresh produce to roasted nuts, to doughnuts to cheeses to blinis – you'll find them, along with wonderful people-watching, at this 1934 landmark. Perfect for families.

Los Angeles County
Museum of Art   Museum

(LACMA; ☎323-857-6000; www.lacma.org; 5905 Wilshire Blvd; adult/child $15/free; ☺11am-5pm Tue & Thu, to 9pm Fri, 10am-7pm Sat & Sun; Ⓟ) LA's premier art museum, LACMA's galleries are stuffed with all the major players – Rembrandt, Cézanne, Magritte, Mary Cassat, Ansel Adams, to name a few – plus several millennia worth of ceramics from China, woodblock prints from Japan, pre-Columbian art, and ancient sculpture from Greece, Rome and Egypt.

Page Museum & La Brea Tar Pits   Museum

(www.tarpits.org; 5801 Wilshire Blvd; adult/child/student & senior $7/2/4.50; ☺9:30am-5pm; Ⓟ🅗) Mammoths and saber-toothed cats used to roam LA's savanna in prehistoric times. We know this because of an archaeological trove of skulls and bones unearthed at La Brea Tar Pits.

Sunset Strip   Street

(Sunset Blvd) A visual cacophony of billboards, giant ad banners and neon signs, the sinuous stretch of Sunset Blvd running between Laurel Canyon and Doheny Dr has been nightlife central since the 1920s.

These days, it seems to be coasting on its legacy. The young, hip and fickle have moved west to Abbot Kinney and east to Downtown, leaving the Strip to the cashed-up suburbanites, though midweek and during awards season the celebs still appear.

Runyon Canyon   Hiking

(www.lamountains.com; 2000 N Fuller Ave; ☺dawn-dusk) A chaparral-draped cut in the Hollywood Hills, this 130-acre public park is as famous for its beautiful, bronzed and buff runners, as it is for the panoramic views from the upper ridge. Follow the wide, partially paved fire road up, then take the smaller track down the canyon where you'll pass the remains of the Runyon estate.

View of Los Angeles from Griffith Observatory
ENZO FIGUERES / GETTY IMAGES ©

Getty Center   Museum

(☎310-440-7300; www.getty.edu; 1200 Getty Center Dr, off I-405 Fwy; ☺10am-5:30pm Tue-Fri & Sun, to 9pm Sat; Ⓟ) **FREE** Richard Meier's wonderfully designed Getty Center is comprised of five buildings that hold collections of manuscripts, drawings, photographs, furniture, decorative arts and a strong assortment of pre-20th-century European paintings. Must-sees include Van Gogh's *Irises*, Monet's *Wheatstacks*, Rembrandt's *The Abduction of Europa* and Titian's *Venus and Adonis*. Don't miss the lovely Cactus Garden on the remote South Promontory for amazing city views.

Malibu

Malibu enjoys near-mythical status thanks to its large celebrity population and the incredible beauty of its coastal mountains, pristine coves, wide sweeps of golden sand and epic waves. Stretched out for 27 miles, there are several small commercial strips, but the heart of town is at the foot of Pepperdine, where you'll find the Malibu Country Mart and the Malibu Civic Center.

The beach is king, of course, and whether you find a sliver of sand among the sandstone rock towers and topless sunbathers at El Matador (32215 Pacific Coast Hwy; parking $8; Ⓟ) or enjoy the wide loamy blonde beaches of Zuma & Westward, you'll have a special afternoon. Topanga Canyon State Park (www.parks.ca.gov; Entrada Rd; per vehicle $10; ☺8am-dusk)

Hollywood

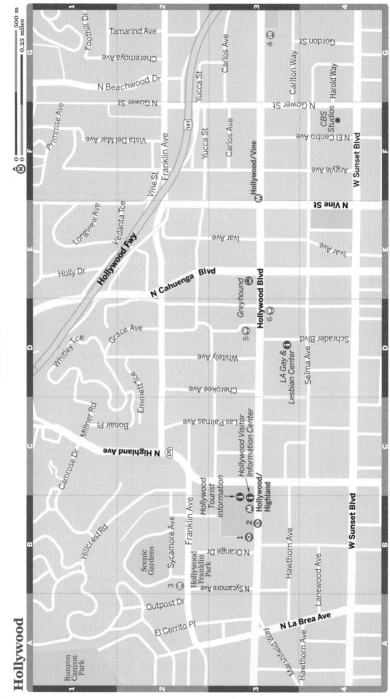

offers 36 miles of hiking trails and the Getty Villa (☑310-430-7300; www.getty.edu; 17985 Pacific Coast Hwy; ◷10am-5pm Wed-Mon; Ⓟ) FREE, a replica of a 1st-century Roman villa, is stocked with Greek and Roman antiquities.

Surfrider Beach   Beach

(26000 Pacific Coast Hwy; Ⓟ) Surf punks descend on this cove that shapes some of the best waves in Southern California. There are several breaks here: the first is well formed for beginners and long boarders, the second and third breaks demand short boards and advanced-level skills. Whichever way you ride, know your etiquette before paddling out.

Santa Monica & Venice

Once the very end of the mythical Route 66, and still a tourist love affair, the Santa Monica Pier (☑310-458-8900; www.santamonicapier.org; ✦) dates back to 1908, is stocked with rides and arcade games and blessed with spectacular views, and is the city's most compelling landmark. After a stroll on the pier, hit the beach (☑310-458-8411; http://www.smgov.net/portals/beach/; ▣ BBB 1). We like the stretch just north of Ocean Park Blvd. Or rent a bike or some skates from Perry's Cafe (☑310-939-0000; www.perryscafe.com; Ocean Front Walk; mountain bikes & Rollerblades per hr/day $10/30, bodyboards per hr/day $7/17; ◷9:30am-5:30pm) and explore the 22-mile South Bay Bicycle Trail.

The Venice Boardwalk (Ocean Front Walk; Venice Pier to Rose Ave; ◷24hr), officially known as Ocean Front Walk, is a wacky carnival alive with altered-states hoola-hoop acrobats, old-timey jazz combos, solo distorted garage rockers and artists – good and bad, but as far as LA experiences go, it's a must. Rent a

bike (☑310-396-2453; 517 Ocean Front Walk; per hr/2hr/day bikes $7/12/20, surfboards $10/20/30, skates $7/12/20) and join the parade, glimpse Muscle Beach (www.musclebeach.net; 1800 Ocean Front Walk; per day $10; ◷8am-7pm May-Sep, to 6pm Oct-Apr) or hit the Skate Park (1800 Ocean Front Walk; ◷dawn-dusk). The Sunday afternoon drum circle is always wild.

⊟ Sleeping

Downtown Los Angeles

Stay   Hotel, Hostel $

(☑213-213-7829; www.stayhotels.com; 640 S Main St; dm/r $39/89; Ⓟ@🛜🛏) Formerly the Hotel Cecil, Stay has marble floors and shared baths, retro furnishings and bedspreads, iPod docks and accent walls. Gleaming shared baths serve just two dorm rooms each and include showers hewn from marble. Rooms all have private baths.

Figueroa Hotel   Historic Hotel $$

(☑800-421-9092, 213-627-8971; www.figueroahotel.com; 939 S Figueroa St; r $148-184, ste $225-265; Ⓟ✳@🛜🛏🐕) It's hard not to be charmed by this rambling owner-operated oasis. Global-chic rooms blend Moroccan mirrors, Iraqi quilts and Kurdish grain-sack floor cushions, with paper lanterns from Chinatown.

Ace Hotel   Hotel $$$

(☑213-623-3233; www.acehotel.com/losangeles; 929 S Broadway Ave; r from $250, stes from $400) Either lovably cool, a bit too hip or a touch self-conscious depending upon your purview, there is no denying that the minds behind Downtown's newest sleep care deeply about their product. Some rooms are cubbybox small, but the 'medium' rooms are doable.

Hollywood & Around

Vibe Hotel   Hostel $

(☑323-469-8600; www.vibehotel.com; 5920 Hollywood Blvd; dm $22-25, r $85-95; Ⓟ@🛜) A funky motel-turned-hostel with both co-ed and female-only dorms – each with a flat screen and kitchenette – and several recently re-done private rooms that sleep three. You'll share space with a happening international crowd.

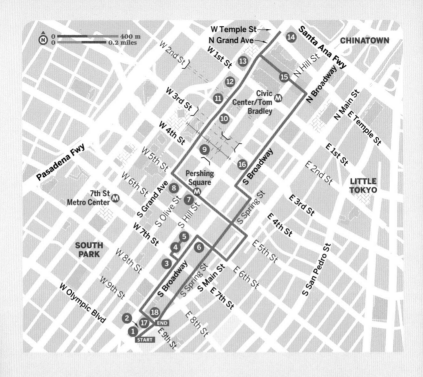

City Walk
Downtown Los Angeles Revealed

START UNITED ARTISTS THEATRE
END WOODSPOON
LENGTH 2.5 MILES; THREE HOURS

Start at the **1 United Artists Theatre**, grab a coffee at the **2 Ace Hotel** next door, then head north on Broadway through the old theater district. This heady mixture of beaux-arts architecture, discount jewelers and new bars, restaurants and shops sums up the Downtown renaissance in just a few short blocks. Take note of the **3 State Theatre** and **4 St Vincent Court**, **5 Los Angeles Theatre** and the **6 Palace Theatre**.

Turn right at 6th St, continue along for two blocks, then turn left onto Main, where you'll see a flowering of new restaurants and bars at nearly every turn. Turn left on 5th St and continue for several blocks, passing

7 Pershing Square and glimpsing the **8 Biltmore Hotel**. At Grand Ave turn right and walk past the **9 Deloitte & Tousche** building, then bisect **10 MOCA** on one side and the **11 Broad** on the other, continuing until you reach the stunning **12 Walt Disney Concert Hall** and the **13 Music Center**. You'll see the **14 Cathedral of Our Lady of Angels** beckoning. Duck inside, then follow the traffic down the steps of **15 Grand Park** until you reach Broadway once more.

Make a right on Broadway, and grab lunch at the **16 Grand Central Market**. Afterward, walk another block south, turn left on 4th St, and then right on lively Spring St, which is dotted with still more cafes and bars. Enjoy the street life and the people-watching until Spring dead ends at Main St, just above 9th St. Say hello to the Cheri Rae at **17 Peace Yoga** (you kind of have to meet her), and hang a right on 9th to Broadway. If you're hungry for dinner by now, grab a table at **18 Woodspoon**.

Magic Castle Hotel
Hotel $$

(☑ 323-851-0800; http://magiccastlehotel.com; 7025 Franklin Ave; r incl breakfast from $174; P ✴ @ 🛜 🏊) Walls at this perennial pleaser are a bit thin, but otherwise it's a charming base of operation with large, modern rooms, exceptional staff and a petite courtyard pool where days start with fresh pastries and gourmet coffee. Enquire about access to the Magic Castle, a fabled members-only magic club in an adjacent Victorian mansion. Parking costs $10.

Pali Hotel
Boutique Hotel $$

(☑ 323-272-4588; www.pali-hotel.com; 7950 Melrose Ave; r from $179; P @ 🛜) We love the rustic wood-paneled exterior, the polished concrete floor in the lobby, the Thai massage spa (just $35 for 30 minutes), and the 32 contemporary rooms with two-tone paint jobs, wall-mounted flat screen and enough room for a sofa, too. Some have terraces. A terrific all-around value.

Standard Hollywood
Hotel $$$

(☑ 323-650-9090; www.standardhotel.com; 8300 Sunset Blvd; r from $235, ste from $335; ✴ @ 🛜 🏊) Kind of yesterday's news but still a good standby, this Sunset Strip haunt has you shacking up in sizable shagadelic rooms with beanbag chairs, orange-tiled bathrooms and Warhol poppy-print curtains. South-facing rooms have the views.

Malibu

Malibu Country Inn
Inn $$

(☑ 310-457-9622; www.malibucountryinn.com; 6506 Westward Beach Rd; r $160-275; P 🛜) Overlooking Westward Beach is this humble shingled inn with an array of fairly large rooms drenched in corny florals. They all have sun patios and some have sea views.

Santa Monica & Venice

HI Los Angeles-Santa Monica
Hostel $

(☑ 310-393-9913; www.hilosangeles.org; 1436 2nd St; dm $38-49, r $99-159; ✴ @ 🛜) Near the beach and promenade, this hostel has an enviable location on the cheap. Its 200 beds in single-sex dorms and bed-in-a-box doubles with shared bathrooms are clean and safe, and there are plenty of public spaces to lounge and surf, but those looking to party are better off in Venice or Hollywood.

Venice Beach Inn & Suites
Boutique Hotel $$

(☑ 310-396-4559; www.venicebeachsuites.com; 1305 Ocean Front Walk; r from $159; P 🛜) This place right on the Boardwalk scores big for its bend-over-backwards staff, and its bevy of beach toys for rent. There are exposed-brick walls, kitchenettes, wood floors and built-in closets. It's ideal for long stays. Kitchen suites are big enough for dinner parties.

Palihouse
Boutique Hotel $$$

(☑ 310-394-1279; www.palihousesantamonica.com; 1001 3rd St; r $279-319, studios $319-379; P ✴ @ 🛜) LA's grooviest new hotel brand (not named Ace) has taken over the 36 rooms, studios and one-bedroom apartments of the historic Embassy Hotel (c 1927). Expect a lobby with terra-cotta floors, beamed ceilings and coffee bar, plus booths and leather sofas on which you can canoodle and surf.

✖ Eating

Downtown Los Angeles

Sushi Gen
Japanese $$

(☑ 213-617-0552; www.sushigen.org; 422 E 2nd St; sushi $11-21; ⏱ 11:15am-2pm & 5:30-9:45pm) Seven chefs stand behind the blond-wood bar, carving thick slabs of melt-in-your-mouth salmon, buttery toro, and a wonderful Japanese snapper, among other staples. The sashimi special at lunch ($18) is a steal. Sushi Gen doesn't do jazzy rolls, and you best come early to grab a seat.

Bestia
Italian $$$

(☑ 213-514-5724; www.bestia.com; 2121 7th Pl; dishes $10-29; ⏱ 6-11pm Sun-Thu, to midnight Fri & Sat) The most sought-after reservation in town can be found at this new and splashy Italian kitchen in the Arts District. The antipasti ranges from crispy lamb pancetta to sea urchin crudo to veal tartare crostino. Did we mention the lamb's heart? Yeah, you may have to leave the vegan at home.

Hollywood & Around

Pingtung
Asian $

(☑ 323-866-1866; www.pingtungla.com; 7455 Melrose Ave; dishes $6-12; ⏱ 11:30am-10:30pm; 🛜) Our new favorite place to eat on Melrose is this Pan-Asian market cafe where the dim sum seaweed and green papaya salads, and rice bowls piled with curried chicken and BBQ beef are all worthy of praise. It has an invit-

Grauman's Chinese Theatre (p90), Hollywood

ing back patio with ample seating, wi-fi and good beer on tap.

Mercado
Mexican $$

(☑ 323-944-0947; www.mercadorestaurant.com; 7910 W 3rd St; dishes $9-26; ⊙ 5-10pm Mon-Wed, to 11pm Thu & Fri, 4-11pm Sat, 10am-3pm & 4-10pm Sun) Terrific *nuevo* Mexican food served in a dining room that is beneath dangling bird-cage chandeliers and anchored by a terrific marble tequila bar. The slow-cooked *carnitas* (pork cubes) melt in your mouth. Mercado also does spit-roast beef and grilled sweet corn, and folds tasty tacos and enchiladas. The Hora Feliz (happy hour) is among the best in the city.

Joan's on Third
Cafe $$

(☑ 323-655-2285; www.joansonthird.com; 8350 W 3rd St; mains $10-16; ⊙ 8am-8pm Mon-Sat, to 7pm Sun; ☑) One of the first market cafes in the LA area is still one of the best. The coffee and pastries are absurdly good and the deli churns out tasty gourmet sandwiches and salads. Hence all the happy people eating alfresco on buzzy 3rd St.

★ Ray's
Modern American $$$

(☑ 323-857-6180; www.raysandstarkbar.com; 5905 Wilshire Blvd; dishes $11-27; ⊙ 11:30am-3pm & 5-10pm Mon-Fri, from 10am Sat & Sun; ☐ MTA 20) Ray's changes the menu twice daily, but if it's offered order the shrimp and grits: it's rich and buttery, afloat with chunks of andouille sausage, okra and two king

prawns. The *burrata* (fresh Italian cheese made from mozzarella and cream) melts with tang, the yellow tail collar is crisp and moist, and the bacon-wrapped rabbit sausage will wow you.

Malibu

Café Habana
Mexican, Cuban $$

(☑ 310-317-0300; www.habana-malibu.com; 3939 Cross Creek Rd; mains $14-22; ⊙ 11am-11pm Sun-Wed, to 1am Thu-Sat; ☑ ☑) A Mexican joint disguised as a Cuban joint with terrific margaritas, sumptuous booths on the heated patio, salsa on the sound system and two dishes that prevail above all else: the shrimp and carne asada tacos. Both come piled with either chili- and lime-sautéed rock shrimp, or cubes of ancho-rubbed and grilled steak.

Santa Monica & Venice

Santa Monica Farmers Markets
Market $

(www.smgov.net/portals/farmersmarket; Arizona Ave, btwn 2nd & 3rd Sts; ⊙ 8:30am-1:30pm Wed, to 1pm Sat; ☑) ✔ You haven't really experienced Santa Monica until you've explored one of its weekly outdoor farmers markets stocked with organic fruits, vegetables, flowers, baked goods and fresh-shucked oysters.

Milo and Olive
Italian $$

(☑ 310-453-6776; www.miloandolive.com; 2723 Wilshire Blvd; dishes $7-20; ⊙ 7am-11pm) We love it for its small-batch wines, incredible pizzas and terrific breakfasts (creamy polenta and poached eggs anyone?), breads and pastries, all of which you may enjoy at the marble bar or shoulder to shoulder with new friends at one of two common tables. It's a cozy, neighborhoody kind of joint; no reservations.

Bar Pintxo
Spanish $$

(🖉 310-458-2012; www.barpintxo.com; 109 Santa Monica Blvd; tapas $4-16, paella $30; ⊙ 4-10pm Mon-Wed, to 11pm Thu, to midnight Fri, noon-midnight Sat, to 10pm Sun) A Barcelona-inspired tapas bar. It's small, it's cramped, it's a bit loud and a lot of fun. Tapas include pork belly braised in duck fat, filet mignon skewers, lamb meatballs and a tremendous seared calamari.

Gjelina
Italian $$$

(🖉 310-450-1429; www.gjelina.com; 1429 Abbot Kinney Blvd; dishes $8-26; ⊙ 11:30am-midnight Mon-Fri, from 9am Sat & Sun; 🖘) Carve out a slip on the communal table between the hipsters and yuppies, or get your own slab of wood on the elegant, tented stone terrace, and dine on imaginative small plates (think raw yellowtail spiced with chili and mint and drenched in olive oil and blood orange), and sensational thin crust, wood-fired pizza. It serves until midnight.

🍸 Drinking & Nightlife

Las Perlas
Bar

(107 E 6th St, Downtown; ⊙ 7pm-2am Mon-Sat, 8pm-2am Sun) With Old Mexico whimsy, a chalkboard menu of more than 80 tequilas and mescals, and friendly barkeeps who mix things such as egg whites, blackberries and port syrup into new-school takes on the margarita, there's a reason we love downtown's best tequila bar. But if you truly want to dig tequila, select a highland variety and sip it neat.

No Vacancy
Bar

(🖉 323-465-1902; www.novacancyla.com; 1727 N Hudson Ave, Hollywood; ⊙ 8pm-2am) An old, shingled Victorian had been converted into LA's hottest night out at research time. Even the entrance is theatrical. You'll follow a rickety staircase into a narrow hall and enter the room of a would-be Madame (dressed in fishnet), who will press a button to reveal another staircase down into the living room and out into a courtyard of mayhem.

Sayers Club
Club

(🖉 323-871-8416; www.sbe.com/nightlife/locations/thesayersclub-hollywood; 1645 Wilcox Ave, Hollywood;

cover varies; ⊙ 8pm-2am Tue, Thu & Fri) When rock royalty such as Prince, established stars like the Black Keys and even movie stars like Joseph Gordon Levitt decide to play secret shows in intimate environs, they find the back room at this brick-house Hollywood nightspot, where the booths are leather, the lighting moody and the music – whether live, or spun by DJs – satisfies.

Bar Marmont
Bar

(🖉 323-650-0575; www.chateaumarmont.com/barmarmont.php; 8171 Sunset Blvd; ⊙ 6pm-2am) Elegant, but not stuck up. Been around, yet still cherished. With high ceilings, molded walls and terrific martinis, the famous, and the wish-they-weres, still flock here. If you time it right, you might see Thom Yorke, or perhaps Lindsey Lohan? Come midweek. Weekends are for amateurs.

Basement Tavern
Bar

(www.basementtavern.com; 2640 Main St, Santa Monica; ⊙ 5pm-2am) This creative speakeasy is our favorite well in Santa Monica. We love it for its cocktails, cozy booths and nightly live-music calendar that features blues, jazz, bluegrass and rock. It gets too busy on weekends, but weeknights can be special.

ℹ Information

Downtown LA Visitor Center (www.discoverlosangeles.com; 800 N Alameda St, Downtown; ⊙ 8:30am-5pm Mon-Fri)

Hollywood Visitor Information Center (🖉 323-467-6412; http://discoverlosangeles.com; Hollywood & Highland complex, 6801 Hollywood Blvd, Hollywood; ⊙ 10am-10pm Mon-Sat, to 7pm Sun) In the Dolby Theatre walkway.

Santa Monica (🖉 800-544-5319; www.santamonica.com; 2427 Main St, Santa Monica) Roving information officers patrol on and around the promenade (on Segways!).

DRIVING IN LOS ANGELES

Unless time is no factor – or money is extremely tight – you're going to want to spend some time behind the wheel, although this means contending with some of the worst traffic in the country. Avoid crossing town at rush hour (7am to 9am and 3:30pm to 7pm).

Parking at motels and cheaper hotels is usually free, while fancier ones charge anywhere from $8 to $40 for the privilege. Valet parking at nicer restaurants and hotels is commonplace with rates ranging from $5 to $10.

Disneyland & Orange County

This diverse county's 789 sq miles, 34 cities and three million people create deep pockets of individuality, beauty and different ways of thinking, keepin' the OC 'real,' no matter one's reality.

Disneyland

The Disneyland Resort is open 365 days a year, though hours vary; check the website. One-day admission to *either* Disneyland or Disney California Adventure (DCA) currently costs $96 for adults and $90 for children aged three to nine. To visit *both* parks in one day costs $135/129 per adult/child on a 'Park Hopper' ticket. A variety of multiday Park Hopper tickets cost up to $305/289 for five days of admission within a two-week period.

Tickets cover all attractions and rides and a variety of parades and shows throughout the day and fireworks most nights in summer and selected times year-round.

Disneyland Park

It's hard to deny the change in atmosphere as you're whisked by tram from the parking lot into the heart of the resort and wide-eyed children lean forward with anticipation. This is their park, but adults who can willingly suspend disbelief may well also give in to the 'magic of Disney'; Uncle Walt's taken care of every detail.

Main Street, U.S.A. — Rides, Attractions

Fashioned after Walt's hometown of Marceline, Missouri, bustling Main Street, U.S.A. resembles the classic turn-of-the-20th-century all-American town. It's an idyllic, relentlessly upbeat representation, complete with barbershop quartet, penny arcades, ice-cream shops and a steam train. The music playing in the background is from American musicals, and there's a flag-retreat ceremony every afternoon.

Great Moments with Mr. Lincoln, a 15-minute Audio-Animatronics presentation on Honest Abe, sits inside the fascinating Disneyland Story exhibit. Nearby, kids love seeing old-school Disney cartoons like *Steamboat Willie* inside Main Street Cinema.

Lording it over Main Street is the iconic Sleeping Beauty Castle, featured on the Disney logo.

Tomorrowland — Rides, Attractions

This 'land' honors three timeless futurists – Jules Verne, HG Wells, and Leonardo da Vinci – while major corporations like Microsoft, Honda, Siemens and HP sponsor futuristic robot shows and interactive exhibits in the Innoventions pavilion.

The retro high-tech monorail glides to a stop in Tomorrowland, its rubber tires traveling a 13-minute, 2.5-mile round-trip route to Downtown Disney. Kiddies will want to shoot laser beams on Buzz Lightyear's Astro Blaster and drive their own miniature cars in the classic Autopia ride (don't worry, they're on tracks).

Then jump aboard the Finding Nemo Submarine Voyage to look for the world's most famous clownfish from within a refurbished submarine and rumble through an underwater volcanic eruption. **Star Tours – The Adventure Continues** clamps you into a Starspeeder shuttle for a wild and bumpy 3D ride through the desert canyons of Tatooine on a space mission with several alternate storylines, so you can ride it again and again. **Space Mountain**, Tomorrowland's signature attraction and one of the USA's best roller coasters, hurtles you into complete darkness at frightening speed. Another classic is Captain EO, a special-effects tribute film starring Michael Jackson.

Fantasyland
Rides, Attractions

Fantasyland is home to **"it's a small world,"** a boat ride past hundreds of creepy Audio-Animatronics children from different cultures all singing the annoying theme song in an astounding variety of languages, joined by Disney characters. Another classic, the **Matterhorn Bobsleds**, mimics a ride down a mountain. The old-school, *Wind in the Willows*–inspired **Mr. Toad's Wild Ride** is a loopy jaunt in an open-air jalopy through London.

Younger kids love whirling around the **Mad Tea Party** teacup ride and **King Arthur Carrousel**, then cavorting with characters in **Mickey's Toontown**, a topsy-turvy mini-metropolis where kiddos can traipse through Mickey and Minnie's houses and dozens of storefronts.

Frontierland
Rides, Attractions

Frontierland's Tom Sawyer Island – the only attraction in the park personally designed by Uncle Walt – has been reimagined as **Pirate's Lair on Tom Sawyer Island**, and now honors Tom in name only. After a raft ride to the island, wander among roving Jack Sparrow–inspired pirates, cannibal cages, ghostly apparitions and buried treasure.

Cruise around the island on the **Mark Twain Riverboat**, a Mississippi-style paddle-wheel boat, or the 18th-century replica sailing ship **Columbia**. The rest of Frontierland gives a nod to the rip-roarin' Old West with a shooting gallery and **Big Thunder Mountain Railroad**, a mining-themed roller coaster.

Adventureland
Rides, Attractions

The hands-down highlight of jungle-themed Adventureland is the safari-style **Indiana Jones™ Adventure**. Enormous Humvee-type vehicles lurch and jerk their way through the wild for spine-tingling re-creations of stunts from the famous film trilogy. Nearby, little ones love climbing the stairways of **Tarzan's Treehouse™**.

Cool down with a **Jungle Cruise** featuring exotic Audio-Animatronics animals from the Amazon, Ganges, Nile and Irrawaddy Rivers. Drop by the **Enchanted Tiki Room** to look at the carvings of Hawaiian gods and goddesses, and animatronic birds singing a corny song so good natured it's hard not to love.

New Orleans Square
Rides, Attractions

New Orleans was Walt's and his wife Lillian's favorite city, and this stunning square has all the charm of the French Quarter minus the marauding drunks. **Pirates of the Caribbean** is the longest ride in Disneyland (17 minutes)

DISNEYLAND RESORT IN...

One Day

Get to **Disneyland** early. Stroll Main Street, U.S.A. toward **Sleeping Beauty Castle**. Enter Tomorrowland to ride **Space Mountain**. In Fantasyland don't miss the classic **"it's a small world"** ride. Race down the **Matterhorn Bobsleds** or take tots to **Mickey's Toontown**. Grab a FASTPASS for the **Indiana Jones™ Adventure** or **Pirates of the Caribbean** before lunching in **New Orleans Square**. Plummet down **Splash Mountain**, then visit the **Haunted Mansion** before the **fireworks** and **Fantasmic!** shows begin.

Two Days

At **Disney California Adventure**, take a virtual hang-gliding ride on **Soarin' Over California** and let kids tackle the **Redwood Creek Challenge Trail** before having fun at **Paradise Pier**, with its roller coaster, Ferris wheel and carnival games. Watch the **Pixar Play Parade**, then explore **Cars Land** or cool off on the **Grizzly River Run**. After dark, drop by **The Twilight Zone Tower of Terror** and **World of Color** show.

TOP TIP: FASTPASS

Disneyland and DCA's FASTPASS system can significantly cut your wait times on many of the most popular rides and attractions.

» At FASTPASS ticket machines – located near entrances to select rides – insert your park entrance ticket. You'll receive an additional ticket showing a return time.

» Show up within the window of time on the ticket and join the ride's FASTPASS line. There'll still be a wait, but it's shorter (typically 15 minutes or less). Hang on to your FASTPASS ticket until you board the ride.

» If you miss the time window printed on your FASTPASS ticket, you can still try joining the FASTPASS line.

and inspired the popular movies. Tawdry pirates and dead buccaneers perch atop their mounds of booty and Jack Sparrow pops up occasionally.

At the Haunted Mansion, 999 happy spirits, goblins and ghosts appear while you ride in a cocoonlike 'Doom Buggy' through webcovered graveyards of dancing skeletons.

Critter Country   Rides, Attractions

Critter Country's main attraction is Splash Mountain, a flume ride that transports you through the story of Brer Rabbit and Brer Bear, based on the controversial 1946 film *Song of the South*. Your picture is taken at the top, and occasionally guests will lift their shirts, leading to the ride's sometime nickname 'Flash Mountain' (naughty photos are deleted!). Just past Splash Mountain, hop in a mobile beehive on The Many Adventures of Winnie the Pooh. Nearby on the Rivers of America, you can paddle Davy Crockett's Explorer Canoes on summer weekends.

Disney California Adventure

Across the plaza from Disneyland, Disney California Adventure (DCA) is a G-rated ode to California. Opened in 2001, it covers more acres than Disneyland and feels less crowded, and it has more modern rides and attractions.

Hollywood Land   Rides, Attractions

California's biggest factory of dreams is presented here in miniature, with soundstages, movable props and – of course – a studio store. The Twilight Zone Tower of Terror is a 13-story drop down an elevator chute situated in a haunted hotel eerily resembling the historic Hollywood Roosevelt Hotel (www.hollywoodroosevelt.com; 7000 Hollywood Blvd; 24hr; P) FREE. From the upper floors of the tower, you'll have views of the Santa Ana mountains, if only for a few heart-pounding seconds.

Less brave children can navigate a taxicab through 'Monstropolis' on the Monsters, Inc: Mike & Sulley to the Rescue! ride heading back toward the street's beginning.

The air-conditioned Muppet Vision 3D theater shows a special-effects film. Learn how to draw like Disney in the Animation Academy, discover how cartoon artwork becomes 3D at the Character Close-Up or simply be amazed by the interactive Sorcerer's Workshop, all housed inside the Animation Building.

Golden State   Rides, Attractions

Golden State highlights California's natural and human achievements. Soarin' Over California is a virtual hang-gliding ride using Omnimax technology that 'flies' you over the Golden Gate Bridge, Yosemite Falls, Lake Tahoe, Malibu and, of course, Disneyland. Keep your senses open for breezes and aromas of the sea, orange groves and pine forests.

Grizzly River Run takes you 'rafting' down a faux Sierra Nevada river – you will get wet, so come when it's warm. Kids can tackle the Redwood Creek Challenge Trail, with its 'Big Sir' redwoods, wooden towers and lookouts, and rock slide and climbing traverses. Get a behind-the-scene looks at what's in the works next for Disneyland's theme parks inside Walt Disney Imagineering Blue Sky Cellar.

Paradise Pier

Rides, Attractions

Paradise Pier, which looks like a combination of all the beachside amusement piers in California, presents carnival rides like California Screamin'; this state-of-the-art roller coaster resembles an old wooden coaster, but it's got a smooth-as-silk steel track.

At Toy Story Midway Mania!, a 4D ride, earn points by shooting at targets while your carnival car swivels and careens through an oversize, old-fashioned game arcade. Mickey's Fun Wheel is a 15-story Ferris wheel where gondolas pitch and yaw in little loops as well as the big one. Silly Symphony Swings is a hybrid carousel with tornado-like chair swings, the pre-school set can ride a more sedate version on the Golden Zephyr and bounce along on the Jumpin' Jellyfish. Goofy's Sky School is a cute and relatively tame cartoon-themed coaster ride.

Cars Land

Rides, Attractions

Based on Disney·Pixar's popular *Cars* movies, this place gives top billing to the wacky Radiator Springs Racers, a race-car ride that bumps and jumps around a track painstakingly decked out like the Great American West. Tractor-towed trailers swing their way around the 'dance floor' at Mater's Junkyard Jamboree. Steer your bumper car (well, bumper tire, to be exact) through Luigi's Flying Tires (enter via the Casa Della Tires shop) or ride along with Route 66–themed gift shops and diners like the tepee-style Cozy Cone Motel.

🛏 Sleeping

Each of the resort's hotels (📞 800-225-2024, reservations 714-956-6425; www.disneyland.com) has a swimming pool with waterslide, kids' activity programs, fitness center, restaurants and bars, business center, and valet or complimentary self-parking for registered guests. Every standard room can accommodate up to five guests and has a mini-refrigerator and a coffeemaker. Look for discounted lodging-and-admission packages and early park entry times for resort guests.

🍴 Eating & Drinking

From Mickey-shaped pretzels ($4) and jumbo turkey legs ($10) to deluxe, gourmet dinners (sky's the limit), there's no shortage of eating options inside the Disney parks, though they're mostly pretty expensive and mainstream. Phone Disney Dining (📞 714-781-3463) to make reservations up to 60 days in advance.

Driving just a couple miles into Anaheim will expand the offerings and price points considerably.

As for drinking, it's tiki to the max and good, clean fun at Trader Sam's Enchanted Tiki Lounge (1150 Magic Way, Disneyland Hotel). Score a personal leather recliner and watch the game on 175-plus screens at ESPN Zone (www.espnzone.com; Downtown Disney), or hear big-name acts at House of Blues (📞 714-778-2583; www.houseofblues.com; Downtown Disney) or jazz at Ralph Brennan's New Orleans Jazz Kitchen (http://rbjazzkitchen.com; Downtown Disney). There's also a 12-screen cinema in Downtown Disney.

❶ Information

Before you arrive, visit **Disneyland Resort** (📞 live assistance 714-781-7290, recorded info 714-781-4565 ; www.disneyland.com) website for up-to-date information.

MOBILE APPS

Disneyland Explorer Official Disney-released app for iPhone and iPad.

TOURIST INFORMATION

Inside the parks, visit Disneyland's City Hall or DCA's guest relations lobby, or just ask any cast member.

Anaheim/Orange County Visitor & Convention Bureau (📞 855-405-5020; www.anaheimoc.org; Anaheim Convention Center) Offers information on countywide lodging, dining and transportation. Convention Center parking is $15.

❶ Getting There & Around

Disneyland Resort is just off I-5 (Santa Ana Fwy), about 30 miles southeast of Downtown LA. All-day parking costs $16 ($20 for oversize vehicles). Enter the 'Mickey & Friends' parking structure from southbound Disneyland Dr, off Ball Rd, and board the free tram to the parks.

Downtown Disney parking, reserved for diners, shoppers and movie-goers, offers the first three hours free.

ORANGE COUNTY BEACHES

Orange County's 42 miles of beaches are a land of gorgeous sunsets, prime surfing, just-off-the-boat seafood and serendipitous discoveries. Whether you're learning to surf the waves in Seal Beach, playing Frisbee oceanside with your pooch, piloting a boat around Newport Harbor, wandering around eclectic art displays in Laguna Beach, or spotting whales on a cruise out of yacht-filled Dana Point harbor, you'll discover that each beach town has its own brand of quirky charm.

Laguna Beach

It's easy to love Laguna: secluded coves, romantic cliffs, azure waves and waterfront parks imbue the city with a Riviera-like feel.

◉ Sights & Activities

With 30 public beaches sprawling along 7 miles of coastline, there's always another stunning view or hidden cove just around the bend. Just look for 'beach access' signs, and be prepared to pass through people's backyards to reach the sand. Rent beach equipment from Main Beach Toys (☑949-494-8808; 150 Laguna Ave; chairs/umbrellas/boards per day $10/10/15; ⊙9am-9pm).

★ Laguna Art Museum   Museum
(☑949-494-8971; www.lagunaartmuseum.org; 307 Cliff Dr; adult/student & senior/child $7/5/free, 1st Thu of month free; ⊙11am-5pm Fri-Tue, to 9pm Thu) This breezy museum has changing exhibitions featuring contemporary Californian artists, and a permanent collection heavy on Californian landscapes, vintage photographs and works by early Laguna bohemians.

Central Beaches   Beaches
Near downtown's village, Main Beach has volleyball and basketball courts, a playground and restrooms. It's Laguna's best beach for swimming. Just north at Picnic Beach, it's too rocky to surf; tide pooling is best. Pick up a tide table at the visitors bureau. (Tide pool etiquette: tread lightly on dry rocks only and don't pick anything up that you find living in the water or on the rocks.)

Above Picnic Beach, the grassy, bluff-top Heisler Park offers vistas of craggy coves and deep-blue sea. Bring your camera – with its palm trees and bougainvillea-dotted bluffs, the scene is definitely one for posterity. A scenic walkway also connects Heisler Park to Main Beach.

North of downtown, Crescent Bay has big hollow waves good for bodysurfing, but parking is difficult; try the bluffs atop the

beach; the views here are reminiscent of the Amalfi Coast.

Diving & Snorkeling
With its coves, reefs and rocky outcroppings, Laguna is one of the best SoCal beaches for diving and snorkeling. Divers Cove just below Heisler Park is part of the Glenn E Vedder Ecological Reserve, an underwater park stretching to the northern border of Main Beach. Check weather and surf conditions (☑949-494-6573) beforehand. Laguna Sea Sports (☑949-494-6965; www.beachcitiesscuba.com; 925 N Coast Hwy; ⊙10am-6pm Mon-Thu, to 7pm Fri, 7am-7pm Sat, 8am-5pm Sun) rents gear and offers classes.

Kayaking
Take a guided kayaking tour of the craggy coves of Laguna's coast – and you might just see a colony of sea lions – with La Vida Laguna (☑949-275-7544; www.lavidalaguna.com; 1257 S Coast Hwy; 2hr guided tour $95). Make reservations at least a day in advance.

Hiking
Surrounded by a green belt – a rarity in SoCal – Laguna has great nature trails for hikes. At Alta Laguna Park, a locals-only park up-canyon from town, the moderate 1.25-mile Park Avenue Nature Trail takes you through fields of spring wildflowers and past panoramic views. Open to hikers and mountain bikers, the 2.5-mile West Ridge Trail follows the ridgeline of the hills above Laguna. To reach the trailheads, take Park Ave to Alta Laguna Blvd then turn left.

⌷ Sleeping

Most lodging in Laguna is on busy Pacific Coast Hwy (called Coast Hwy here), so expect traffic noise; bring earplugs or ask for a room away from the road.

★ The Tides Inn   Motel $$
(☑888-777-2107, 949-494-2494; www.tideslaguna.com; 460 N Coast Hwy; r $175-285; P❄🛜🐾🏊) A bargain for Laguna, especially considering its convenient location just three long blocks north of the village. It feels rather upscale, with plush bedding, beachy-keen decor and inspirational quotes painted into each room. Each room is different; some have kitchenettes. Shared facilities include saltwater pool, barbecue grill and a fireplace for toasting marshmallows. Pet fee $25 to $40.

✕ Eating & Drinking

There are almost as many watering holes in downtown's village as there are art galleries. Most cluster along S Coast Hwy and Ocean Ave, making for an easy pub crawl. If you drink, don't drive; local cops take DUI's very seriously.

Taco Loco   Mexican $

(http://tacoloco.net; 640 S Coast Hwy; mains $3-14; ⊙11am-midnight Sun-Thu, to 2am Fri & Sat; 🖉) Throw back Coronas with the surfers while watching the passersby at this Mexican sidewalk cafe. Taco, quesadilla and nacho options seem endless: blackened calamari or tofu, swordfish, veggie (potato, mushroom, tofu) and shrimp to name a few. For dessert: hemp brownies. Order at the counter, dude.

House of Big Fish & Cold Beer   Seafood $$

(🖉949-715-4500; www.houseofbigfish.com; 540 S Coast Hwy; mains $7-15; ⊙11:30am-10:30pm) The name says it all (what else do you need?): Hawaii-style *poke* (marinated raw fish), Baja-style fish tacos, coconut shrimp and the fresh catch o' the day. There are dozens of beers with about one-third from California. Make reservations, or wait, like, forever.

❶ Information

Visit Laguna Beach Visitors Center (🖉949-497-9229; www.lagunabeachinfo.com; 381 Forest Ave; ⊙10am-5pm; 🖳) Helpful staff, bus schedules, restaurant menus and free brochures on everything from hiking trails to self-guided walking tours.

❶ Getting There & Away

From I-405, take Hwy 133 (Laguna Canyon Rd) southwest. Hwy 1 goes by several names in Laguna Beach: south of Broadway, downtown's main street, it's called South Coast Hwy; north of Broadway it's North Coast Hwy. Locals also call it Pacific Coast Hwy or just PCH.

Around Laguna Beach

★ Mission San Juan Capistrano   Church

(🖉949-234-1300; www.missionsjc.com; 26801 Ortega Hwy, San Juan Capistrano; adult/child $9/6; ⊙9am-5pm) Padre Junipero Serra founded the mission on November 1, 1776, and tended it personally for many years. Particularly moving are the towering remains of the Great Stone Church, almost completely destroyed by a powerful earthquake on Decem-

Newport Beach
GARY CRABBE / GETTY IMAGES ©

ber 8, 1812. The Serra Chapel – whitewashed outside with restored frescoes inside – is believed to be the oldest existing building in California (1778). Plan on spending at least an hour poking around the sprawling mission's tiled roofs, covered arches, lush gardens, fountains and courtyards – including the padre's quarters, soldiers' barracks and the cemetery. Admission includes a worthwhile free audio tour with interesting stories narrated by locals.

Newport Beach

There are really three Newport Beaches demographics: wealthy Bentley- and Porsche-driving yachtsmen and their trophy wives; surfers and stoners who populate the beachside dives and live for the perfect wave; and everyone else trying to live day-to-day, chow on seafood and enjoy glorious sunsets. Somehow, these diverse communities all seem to live – mostly – harmoniously.

◉ Sights & Activities

Balboa Fun Zone   Amusement Park

(www.thebalboafunzone.com; 600 E Bay Ave; ⊙Ferris wheel 11am-8pm Sun-Thu, to 9pm Fri, to 10pm Sat)

On the harbor side of Balboa Peninsula, the Fun Zone has delighted locals and visitors since 1936. There's a small Ferris wheel ($4 per ride, where Ryan and Marissa shared their first kiss on *The OC*), arcade games, touristy shops and restaurants, and frozen banana stands (just like the one in the TV sit-com *Arrested Development*). The landmark 1905 Balboa Pavilion is beautifully illuminated at night.

Balboa Peninsula   Beaches

Four miles long but less than a half mile wide, the Balboa Peninsula has a white-sand beach on its ocean side, great people-watching and countless stylish homes.

Hotels, restaurants and bars cluster around the peninsula's two famous piers: Newport Pier near the western end and Balboa Pier at the eastern end. Near Newport Pier, several shops rent umbrellas, beach chairs, volleyballs and other necessities. For swimming, families will find a more relaxed atmosphere and calmer waves at Mothers Beach (10th St & 18th St).

Surfing

Surfers flock to the breaks at the small jetties surrounding the Newport Pier. At the tip of Balboa Peninsula, by the West Jetty, the Wedge is a bodysurfing, bodyboarding and knee-boarding spot famous for its perfectly hollow waves that can swell up to 30ft high. Warning: locals can be territorial, and newcomers should head a few blocks west.

🛏 Sleeping

A Newport stay ain't cheap, but outside peak season, rates listed here often drop 40% or more.

Newport Channel Inn   Motel $$

(☎800-255-8614, 949-642-3030; www.newport channelinn.com; 6030 W Coast Hwy; r $129-199; P❄🛜) The ocean is just across Pacific Coast Hwy from this spotless 30-room, two-story 1960s-era motel. Other perks include large rooms with microwaves and mini-fridges, a big common sundeck, beach equipment for loan and genuinely friendly owners with lots of local knowledge. Enjoy a vacation-lodge vibe under the A-frame roof of Room 219, which sleeps up to seven.

Newport Dunes Waterfront
RV Resort & Marina   Cabins, Camping $$

(☎949-729-3863, 800-765-7661; www.newportdunes. com; 1131 Back Bay Dr; campsites from $55, studios/ cottages from $150/200; P@🛜❄🐾) RVs and tents aren't required for a stay at this upscale campground: two dozen tiny A-frame studios and one-bedroom cottages are available, all within view of Newport Bay. A fitness center and walking trails, kayak rentals, board games, family bingo, ice-cream socials, horseshoe and volleyball tournaments, an outdoor pool and playground, and summertime movies on the beach await.

🍴 Eating & Drinking

⭐ Bear Flag Fish Company   Seafood $$

(☎949-673-3434; www.bearflagfishco.com; 407 31st St, Newport Beach; mains $8-15; ⏱11am-9pm Tue-Sat, to 8pm Sun & Mon; 🚗) This squat glass box is *the* place for generously sized, grilled and panko-breaded fish tacos, ahi burritos, spankin' fresh ceviche and oysters. Pick out what you want from the ice-cold display cases, then grab a picnic-table seat.

Newport Beach Brewing Company   Brewpub

(www.newportbeachbrewingcompany.com; 2920 Newport Blvd; ⏱11:30am-11pm Sun-Thu, to 1am Fri & Sat; 🍴) The town's only microbrewery (try the signature Newport Beach Blonde or Bisbee's ESB), 'Brewco' is a laid-back place to catch the big game or just kick it over burgers, pizzas and fried fare with your buds after a day at the beach.

❶ Information

Explore Newport Beach (www.

visitnewportbeach.com; 401 Newport Center Dr, Fashion Island, Atrium Court, 2nd fl; ⏱10am-9pm Mon-Fri, to 7pm Sat, to 6pm Sun) The city's official visitor center.

Huntington Beach

With consistently good waves, surf shops, a surf museum, beach bonfires, a canine-friendly beach and a sprinkling of hotels and restaurants with killer views, HB is an awesome place for sun, surf and sand.

Hawaiian-Irish surfing star George Freeth gave demonstrations here in 1914, and the city has been a surf destination ever since, with the trademarked nickname 'Surf City, USA' (Santa Cruz lost that fight, sorry). The sport is big business, with a Surfing Walk of Fame (www.hsssurf.com/shof) and test-marketing for surf products and clothing.

◉ Sights

Huntington Pier   Historic Site
(⏰ 5am-midnight) The 1853ft-long Huntington Pier has been here – in one form or another – since 1904. On the pier, rent a fishing pole from Let's Go Fishin' bait and tackle shop.

International Surfing Museum   Museum
See p47.

Huntington City Beach   Beach
(⏰ 5am-midnight) One of SoCal's best beaches. Surrounding the pier at the foot of Main St, it gets packed on summer weekends with surfers, volleyball players, swimmers and families. Check at the visitor center for dog-friendly beaches and parks.

By night, volleyball games give way to beach bonfires. Stake out one of the 1000 cement fire rings early in the day, and you can buy firewood from concessionaires.

⚓ Activities

If you forgot to pack beach gear, you can rent umbrellas, beach chairs, volleyballs, bikes and other essentials from Zack's Pier Plaza. Just south of the pier on the Strand, friendly Dwight's Beach Concession (201 Pacific Coast Hwy), around since 1932, rents bikes, boogie boards, umbrellas and chairs. Surfing in HB is competitive. If you're a novice, take lessons, or risk annoying the locals. Explore the coast while zipping along the 8.5-mile paved recreational path from Huntington State Beach north to Bolsa Chica State Beach. Rent beach cruisers ($10/30 per hour/day) or tandem bikes ($18/50) at Zack's Pier Plaza.

🛏 Sleeping

Huntington Surf Inn   Motel $$
(☎ 714-536-2444; www.huntingtonsurfinn.com; 720 Pacific Coast Hwy; r $159-209; 🅿 🛜) You're paying for location at this two-story motel just south of Main St and across from the beach.

Nine of its rooms were recently redesigned by surf company Hurley in conjunction with surfers – cool, brah. There's a small common deck area with a beach view.

★ Shorebreak Hotel   Boutique Hotel $$$
(☎ 714-861-4470; www.shorebreakhotel.com; 500 Pacific Coast Hwy, Huntington Beach; r $189-495; 🅿 ❄ @ 🛜 🐕) Stow your surfboard (lockers provided) as you head inside HB's hippest hotel, a stone's throw from the pier. The Shorebreak has a surf concierge, a fitness center and yoga studio, beanbag chairs in the lobby, and rattan and hardwood furniture in geometric-patterned rooms. Have sunset cocktails on the upstairs deck at Zimzala restaurant. Parking is $27.

🍴 Eating & Drinking

It's easy to find a bar in HB. Walk up Main St and you'll spot them all.

Sancho's Tacos   Mexican $
(☎ 714-536-8226; www.sanchostacos.com; 602 Pacific Coast Hwy; mains $3-10; ⏰ 8am-9pm Mon-Sat, to 8pm Sun) There's no shortage of taco stands in HB, but locals are fiercely dedicated to Sancho's, across from the beach. This two-room shack with patio grills flounder, shrimp and tri-tip to order. Trippy Mexican-meets-skater art.

Duke's   Seafood, Hawaiian $$
(☎ 714-374-6446;   www.dukeshuntington.com; 317 Pacific Coast Hwy; lunch $7-16, dinner $19-32; ⏰ 11:30am-2:30pm Tue-Fri, 10am-2pm Sun, 5-9pm Tue-Sun) It may be touristy, but this Hawaiian-themed restaurant – named after surfing legend Duke Kahanamoku – is a kick. With unbeatable views of the beach, a long list of fresh fish and a healthy selection of sassy cocktails, it's a primo spot to relax and show off your tan.

ℹ Information

Visitors Bureau (☎ 800-729-6232; www.surfcityusa.com) Main St (☎ 714-969-3492; www.surfcityusa.com; 2nd fl, 301 Main St; ⏰ 9am-5pm); Pier Plaza (www.surfcityusa.com; Pier Plaza; ⏰ 11am-7pm) Hard-to-spot upstairs office on Main St provides maps and information, but the Pier Plaza booth is more convenient.

San Diego

San Diego bursts with world-famous attractions for the entire family, a bubbling downtown and beaches ranging from ritzy to raucous, and America's most perfect weather.

◉ Sights

San Diego's Zoo is a highlight of any trip to California and should be a high priority for first-time visitors. It's in Balboa Park, which itself is packed with museums and gardens.

To visit the zoo, all 14 museums, half-dozen botanical gardens and more would take days; plan your trip at the Balboa Park Visitors Center (☑619-239-0512; www.balboapark.org; House of Hospitality, 1549 El Prado; ⊙9:30am-4:30pm). Pick up a map (suggested donation $1) and the opening schedule.

★ San Diego Zoo   Zoo

(☑619-231-1515; www.sandiegozoo.org; 2920 Zoo Dr; 1-day pass adult/child from $46/36; 2-visit pass to Zoo and/or Safari Park adult/child $82/64; ⊙9am-9pm mid-Jun–early Sep, to 5pm or 6pm early Sep–mid-Jun; P🚼) 🅿 This justifiably famous zoo is one of SoCal's biggest attractions, showing more than 3000 animals representing over 800 species in a beautifully landscaped setting, typically in enclosures that replicate their natural habitats. Its sister park is San Diego Zoo Safari Park in northern San Diego County.

Arrive early, as many of the animals are most active in the morning – though many perk up again in the afternoon. Pick up a map at the entrance to the zoo to find your own favorite exhibits.

Balboa Park Museums   Museum

(www.balboapark.org; Balboa Park; Passport (allows entry to each museum within 1 week) adult/child $53/29, Stay for the Day (5 museums in 1 day) $43; Combo Pass (Passport plus zoo) adult/child $89/52) Among the park's museums, standouts are the Reuben H Fleet Science Center (☑619-238-1233; www.rhfleet.org; 1875 El Prado; adult/child $13/11, incl Giant Dome Theater $17/14; ⊙10am-5pm Mon-Thu, to 6pm Fri-Sun; 🚼), with its Giant Dome movie presentations; the San Diego Natural History Museum (☑619-232-3821; www.sdnhm.org; 1788 El Prado; adult/child $17/11; ⊙10am-5pm; 🚼); the San Diego Museum of Art (SDMA; ☑619-232-7931; www.sdmart.org; 1450 El Prado; adult/child $12/4.50; ⊙10am-5pm Mon-Tue & Thu-Sat, from noon Sun, also 5-9pm Thu Jun-Sep), the city's largest; the Timken Museum of Art (☑619-239-5548; www.timkenmuseum.org; 1500 El Prado; ⊙10am-4:30pm Tue-Sat, from 1:30pm Sun) **FREE**, with works by masters such as Rembrandt, Rubens, El Greco, Cézanne and Pissarro; and the Mingei International Museum (☑619-239-0003; www.mingei.org; 1439 El Prado; adult/child $8/5; ⊙10am-5pm Tue-Sun; 🚼), featuring folk crafts from around the world.

Other, museums include the San Diego Model Railroad Museum (☑619-696-0199; www.sdmrm.org; Casa de Balboa, 1649 El Prado; adult/child under 6yr $8/free; ⊙11am-4pm Tue-Fri, to 5pm Sat & Sun; 🚼), the Museum of Photographic Arts (☑619-238-7559; www.mopa.org; Casa de Balboa, 1649 El Prado; adult/

student/child $8/6/free; ⊙10am-5pm Tue-Sun, to 9pm Thu late May–Aug), the Spanish Village Art Center Artist Colony (⊙11am-4pm) FREE and the Marie Hitchcock Puppet Theater (☑619-685-5990; www.balboaparkpuppets.com; Balboa Park; admission $5.50; ⊙11am, 1pm & 2:30pm Wed-Sun late May-early Sep, shorter hours early Sep-late May; ♿).

Downtown San Diego

Downtown San Diego was a rough place in the 19th century, full of saloons, gambling joints, bordellos and opium dens. By the 1960s it had declined to a skid row of flop-houses and bars.

But thanks to strong bones and a local preservation and restoration movement, historic buildings have been restored and collectively renamed the Gaslamp Quarter, now full of restaurants, nightspots and theaters amid 19th-century-style street lamps, trees and brick sidewalks. A few 'adult entertainment' shops, and a fair number of homeless folks serve as reminders of the old days.

See the Gaslamp's early history at the Gaslamp Museum & William Heath Davis House (www.gaslampquarter.org; 410 Island Ave; adult/senior & student $5/4, walking tour $10/8; ⊙10am-6pm Tue-Sat, 9am-3pm Sun, walking tour 11am Sat), San Diego Chinese Historical

Museum (404 3rd Ave; ⊙10:30am-4pm Tue-Sun) FREE and US Grant Hotel (☑619-232-3121; 326 Broadway).

Next door, the East Village is a hub of exciting contemporary architecture like the baseball stadium Petco Park (☑619-795-5011; www.padres.com; 100 Park Blvd; tours adult/child/senior $12/8/9; ⊙tours 10:30am & 12:30pm Sun-Fri, 10:30am, 12:30pm & 3pm off season; ♿) and the stunning new Main Library (www.sandiego.gov/public-library; 330 Park Blvd; ⊙noon-8pm Mon, Wed & Fri, 9:30am-5:30pm Tue & Thu, 9:30am-2:30pm Sat, 1-5pm Sun), both open for visitors.

Museum of Contemporary Art   Museum
(MCASD Downtown; ☑858-454-3541; www.mcasd.org; 1001 Kettner Blvd; adult/child under 25yr/senior $10/free/5, 5-7pm 3rd Thu each month free; ⊙11am-5pm Thu-Tue, to 7pm 3rd Thu each month) This museum brings an ever-changing variety of innovative artwork to San Diegans, in the downtown location and the La Jolla branch. Across from the main building, a slickly renovated section of San Diego's train station houses permanent works by Jenny Holzer and Richard Serra. Tickets are valid for seven days in all locations.

★New Children's Museum   Museum
(www.thinkplaycreate.org; 200 W Island Ave; admission $10; ⊙noon-4pm Sun, 1am-4pm Mon &

SAN DIEGO IN...

It's easy to spend most of a week in San Diego, but if your time is limited, here's a whirlwind itinerary. Things will go more smoothly if you've got access to a car.

One Day

Rub elbows with the locals over breakfast in the Gaslamp Quarter then ramble around Old Town State Historic Park for a bit of history before a Mexican lunch. Devote the afternoon to the San Diego Zoo, which is among the world's best, and if time permits visit some of the museums or gardens in graceful Balboa Park. For dinner and a night out on the town, head to the hip East Village or back to the Gaslamp Quarter, where many restaurants have terrace seating for people-watching, and the partying ranges from posh to raucous.

Two Days

Take the ferry to Coronado for a sea-view breakfast at the Hotel del Coronado, then enjoy the California beach scene at Mission and Pacific Beaches. La Jolla beckons this afternoon: explore Torrey Pines State Reserve, Birch Aquarium at Scripps, kayak the sea caves, try a glider ride or head to La Jolla Village to browse the 1920s Spanish Revival landmarks and boutiques. As the sun begins its descent over the ocean, head to Del Mar, where you can cheer from, or snuggle at, one of the restaurants on the roof of Del Mar Plaza (1555 Camino Del Mar) while the sky turns brilliant orange and fades to black.

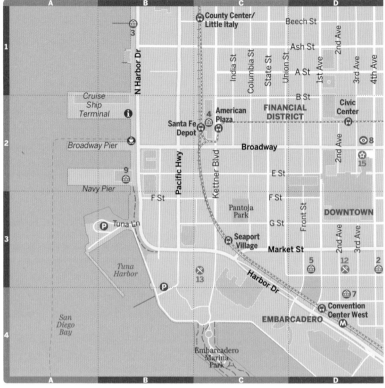

Wed-Sat; ☷) This interactive children's museum opened in 2008. Artists have designed installations so that tykes can learn principles of movement and physics while simultaneously being exposed to art and working out the ants in their pants. Exhibits change roughly every 18 months, so there's always something new.

Old Town

In 1821, when California was under Mexican rule, the area below the Presidio (fort) became the first official civilian Mexican settlement in California: the Pueblo de San Diego.

In 1968 the area was named Old Town State Historic Park (☑619-220-5422; www.parks.ca.gov; 4002 Wallace St; ☺visitor center & museums 10am-4pm Oct-Apr, to 5pm May-Sep; 🅿☷) FREE, archaeological work began, and the few surviving original buildings were restored.

There's the park visitor center and an excellent history museum in the Robinson-Rose House at the southern end of the plaza. The Whaley House (☑619-297-7511; www.whaleyhouse.org; 2476 San Diego Ave; adult/child before 5pm $6/4, after 5pm $10/5; ☺10am-10pm late May-early Sep, 10am-5pm Mon-Tue, to 10pm Thu-Sat early Sep-late May) is the city's oldest brick building and nearby is El Campo Santo (San Diego Ave btwn Arista & Conde Sts), an 1849 cemetery for some 20 souls with their biographies on signage. The Junipero Serra Museum (☑619-297-3258; www.sandiegohistory.org; 2727 Presidio Dr; adult/child $6/3; ☺10am-4pm Sat & Sun mid-Sep–mid-May, to 5pm Sat & Sun mid-May–mid-Sep; 🅿☷) is named for the Spanish *padre* who established the first Spanish settlement in California, in 1769, and has artifacts of the city's Mission and Rancho Periods. The Mission Basilica San Diego de Alcalá (☑619-281-8449; www.missionsandiego.com; 10818 San Diego

Downtown San Diego

⊚ Sights

🛏 Sleeping

🍴 Eating

🍷 Drinking & Nightlife

🎭 Entertainment

admiral's war room, brig and primary flight control.

★ **Maritime Museum**   Museum

(☎619-234-9153; www.sdmaritime.org; 1492 N Harbor Dr; adult/child $16/8; ⊙9am-9pm late May-early Sep, to 8pm early Sep-late May; ⊛) Look for the 100ft-high masts of the iron-hulled square-rigger *Star of India*, a tall ship that plied the England–India trade route.

Coronado

Across the bay from Downtown San Diego, Coronado is an escape from the jumble of the city. The story of Coronado is in many ways the story of the Hotel del Coronado (see p18), opened in 1888 and the centerpiece of one of the West Coast's most fashionable getaways. Coronado's visitors center doubles as the Coronado Museum of History and Art and offers 90-minute historical walking tours. Coronado Municipal Beach (parking up to $8; ⊛) is consistently ranked in America's top 10. Four-and-a-half miles south of Coronado Village is Silver Strand State Beach (☎619-435-5184; www.parks.ca.gov; 5000 Hwy 75; per car $10-15;

Mission Rd; adult/child $3/1; ⊙9am-4:30pm; P) eventually moved 7 miles away and is worth a visit.

Embarcadero & the Waterfront

South and west of the Gaslamp Quarter, San Diego's well-manicured waterfront promenades stretch along Harbor Dr, home to excellent museums of naval and sea life, and are perfect for strolling or jogging (or watching well-built members of the US Navy doing same, if that's your thing!).

★ **USS Midway Museum**   Museum

(☎619-544-9600; www.midway.org; 910 N Harbor Dr; adult/child $20/10; ⊙10am-5pm, last entry 4pm; P⊛) The permanent home of this giant aircraft carrier (1945–91). On the flight deck, walk right up to some 25 restored aircraft. Admission includes an audio tour to

Ocean Beach

). Both have warm, calm water, perfect for swimming and good for families.

Mission Bay & Mission & Pacific Beaches

The big ticket attraction around Mission Bay is SeaWorld, while the nearby Mission, Ocean and Pacific Beaches are the SoCal of the movies.

SeaWorld San Diego
Theme Park

(☑ 800-257-4268; www.seaworldsandiego.com; 500 SeaWorld Dr; adult/child 3-9yr $84/78; ⊙ daily; Ⓟ 📱) SeaWorld opened in San Diego in 1964 and remains one of California's most popular theme parks. Many visitors spend the whole day here, shuttling between shows, rides and exhibits – you can pick up a map to plan your day around scheduled events.

Mission Bay
Outdoor Activities

Just east of Mission and Pacific Beaches is this 7-sq-mile playground, with 27 miles of shore-line and 90 acres of parks on islands, coves and peninsulas. Sailing, windsurfing and kayaking dominate northwest Mission Bay, while waterskiers zip around Fiesta Island. Kite flying is popular in Mission Bay Park, beach volleyball on Fiesta Island, and there's delightful cycling and inline skating on bike paths.

🏃 Activities

Surfing

Rental rates vary, but figure on soft boards from $15/45 per hour/day; wetsuits cost $7/28. Equipment and/or lessons are available from outfits including Pacific Beach Surf School (☑ 858-373-1138; www.pbsurfshop. com; 4150 Mission Blvd; ⊙ store 9am-7pm, lessons hourly until 4pm) and Bob's Mission Surf (☑ 858-483-8837; www.missionsurf.com; 4320 Mission Blvd, Pacific Beach).

Fishing

The most popular public fishing piers are Imperial Beach Pier, Embarcadero Fishing Pier, Shelter Island Fishing Pier, Ocean Beach Pier and Crystal Pier at Pacific Beach. Generally the best pier fishing is from April to October.

Kayaking

Ocean kayaking is a good way to observe sea life, and explore cliffs and caves inaccessible from land. Guided tours and lessons are available from Family Kayak (☑ 619-282-3520; www.familykayak.com; adult/child from $44/18; ⬦).

Whale-Watching

Gray whales pass San Diego from mid-December to late February on their way south to Baja California, and again in mid-March on their way back up to Alaskan waters. Visit Cabrillo National Monument (p18) to spy whales from land, or go on a tour.

- - - - - - - - - - - - - - - - - - - -

🛏 Sleeping

San Diego Tourism runs a room-reservation line (☑ 800-350-6205; www.sandiego.org).

USA Hostels San Diego   Hostel $
(☑ 619-232-3100, 800-438-8622; www.usahostels. com; 726 5th Ave; dm/r with shared bath incl breakfast from $33/79; @ ⑤) Lots of charm and color at this convivial hostel in a former Victorian-era hotel. Look for cheerful rooms, a full kitchen, a communal lounge for chilling and in-house parties and beach barbecues. Rates include linens, lockers and pancakes for breakfast. And it's smack-dab in the middle of Gaslamp nightlife. No air-con.

Hotel Solamar   Boutique, Contemporary $$
(☑ 877-230-0300, 619-531-8740; www.hotelsolamar. com; 435 6th Ave; r $169-299; P ✱ @ ⑤ ⬦) A great compromise in the Gaslamp: hip style that needn't break the bank. Lounge beats play in the background as you gaze at the Downtown skyscrapers from the pool deck and bar, and rooms have sleek lines and nautical blue and neo-rococo accents for a touch of fun. It has a fitness center, in-room yoga kit, loaner bikes and a nightly complimentary wine hour. Parking costs $41.

La Pensione Hotel   Boutique Hotel $$
(www.lapensionehotel.com; 606 W Date St; r $110-159; P ✱ ⑤; ☐ 5, ⬦ Pacific Hwy & W Cedar St) Despite the name, Little Italy's La Pensione isn't a pension but an intimate, friendly, recently renovated hotel of 68 rooms – around a frescoed courtyard – with queen-size beds

and private bathrooms. It's only steps from the neighborhood's dining, cafes and galleries, and is within walking distance of most Downtown attractions. There's an attractive cafe downstairs. Parking is $15.

Cosmopolitan Hotel   Historic B&B $$
(☑ 619-297-1874; www.oldtowncosmopolitan.com; 2660 Calhoun St; r incl breakfast $150-250; ☉ front desk 9am-9pm; P ⑤) Right in Old Town State Park, this creaky, 10-room hotel from 1870 has oodles of charm, antique furnishings, and a restaurant downstairs for lunch and dinner. Don't go expecting modern conveniences like phones and TV, though there's free wi-fi. Breakfast is a simple affair based on coffee and scones. Free parking.

US Grant Hotel   Luxury $$$
(☑ 619-232-3121, 800-237-5029; www.starwood. com; 326 Broadway; r from $249; P ✱ @ ⑤) This 1910 hotel was built as the fancy city counterpart to the Hotel del Coronado and has hosted everyone from Albert Einstein to Harry Truman. Today's quietly flashy lobby combines chocolate-brown and ocean-blue accents, and rooms boast original artwork on the headboards. Parking costs $39.

- - - - - - - - - - - - - - - - - - - -

🍴 Eating & Drinking

Café 222   Breakfast $
(☑ 619-236-9902; www.cafe222.com; 222 Island Ave; mains $7-11; ☉ 7am-1:30pm) Downtown's favorite breakfast place serves renowned peanut butter and banana French toast; buttermilk, orange-pecan or granola pancakes; and eggs in scrambles or Benedicts. It also sells lunchtime sandwiches and salads, but we always go for breakfast (available until closing).

Cucina Urbana   Californian, Italian $$
(☑ 619-239-2222; 505 Laurel St, Bankers Hill; lunch $10-23, dinner $12-28; ☉ 11:30am-2pm Tue-Fri, 5-9pm Sun & Mon, 5-10pm Tue-Thu, 5pm-midnight Fri & Sat) In this corner place with modern rustic ambience, business gets done, celebrations get celebrated and friends hug and kiss over refined yet affordable Cal Ital cooking. Look for short rib pappardelle, pizzas like foraged mushroom with taleggio cheese and braised leeks, and smart cocktails and local 'brewskies.'

Urban Solace   Californian $$
(☑ 619-295-6464; www.urbansolace.net; 3823 30th St, North Park; mains lunch $10-23, dinner $17-27; ☉ 11:30am-10pm Mon-Thu, to 11pm Fri, 5-11pm Sat,

5-9pm Sun) North Park's young hip gourmets revel in creative comfort food here: bluegrass burger; 'not your mama's' meatloaf of ground lamb, fig, pine nuts and feta; 'duckaroni' (mac 'n' cheese with duck confit); and chicken and dumplings. The setting is surprisingly chill for such great eats; maybe it's the cocktails like mojitos made with bourbon.

Puesto at the Headquarters   Mexican $$

(☑ 610-233-8800; www.eatpuesto.com; 789 W Harbor Dr, The Headquarters; mains $11-19; ☺ 11am-10pm) This upscale eatery serves Mexican street food that knocked our *zapatos* off: innovative takes on traditional tacos like chicken (with hibsicus, chipotle, pineapple and avocado) and some out-there fillings like potato soy chorizo. Other highlights: crab guacamole, *barbacoa* short ribs (braised in chili sauce) and Mexican street bowl, ie tropical fruits with chili, sea salt and lime.

Prado   Californian $$$

(☑ 619-557-9441; www.pradobalboa.com; House of Hospitality, 1549 El Prado; mains lunch $12-21, dinner $22-35; ☺ 11:30am-3pm Mon-Fri, from 11am Sat & Sun, 5-9pm Sun & Tue-Thu, to 10pm Fri & Sat) In one of San Diego's most beautiful dining rooms, feast on Cal-eclectic cooking by one of San Diego's most renowned chefs: bakery sandwiches, chicken and orecchiette pasta, and pork prime rib. Go for a civilized lunch on the verandah or for afternoon cocktails and appetizers in the bar.

Bang Bang   Bar

(www.bangbangsd.com; 526 Market St; ☺ closed Mon) Beneath lantern-light, the Gaslamp's hottest new spot hosts local and world-known DJs, and serves sushi and Asian small plates to accompany imaginative cocktails (some in giant goblets meant for sharing with your posse). Bathrooms are shrines to Ryan Gosling and Hello Kitty: in a word, awesome.

- - - - - - - - - - - - - - - - - - - -

☆ Entertainment

Check out the San Diego *City Beat* or *UT San Diego* for the latest movies, theater, galleries and music gigs around town. Arts Tix (☑ 858-381-5595; www.sdartstix.com; Lyceum Theatre, 79 Horton Plaza), in a kiosk near Westfield Horton Plaza, has half-price tickets for many shows.

❶ Information

International Visitor Information Center

(☑ 619-236-1212; www.sandiego.org; 1140 N Harbor Dr; ☺ 9am-5pm Jun-Sep, to 4pm Oct-May) Across from the B St Cruise Ship Terminal, helpful staff offer detailed neighborhood maps, sell discounted tickets to attractions and maintain a hotel reservation hotline.

San Diego Tourism (www.sandiego.org) Search hotels, sights, dining, rental cars and more, and make reservations.

❶ Getting There & Away

Allow two hours from LA in non-peak traffic. With traffic, it's anybody's guess.

Gardens, Balboa Park

California Driving Guide

With jaw-dropping scenery and one of the USA's most comprehensive highway networks, California is an all-star destination for a road trip any time of year.

Driving Fast Facts

- **Right or left?** Drive on the right
- **Legal driving age** 16
- **Top speed limit** 70mph (some interstate and state highways)
- **Best bumper sticker** Mystery Spot, Santa Cruz

DRIVER'S LICENSE & DOCUMENTS

Out-of-state and international visitors may legally drive a car in California for up to 12 months with their home driver's license. If you're driving into the USA from Canada or Mexico, bring your vehicle's registration papers, liability insurance and home driver's license; an International Driving Permit (IDP) is a good supplement but isn't currently required.

If you're from overseas, an IDP will have more credibility with traffic police and will simplify the car-rental process, especially if your license doesn't have a photo or isn't written in English. International automobile associations can issue IDPs, valid for one year, for a fee. Always carry your home license together with the IDP.

The American Automobile Association (AAA) has reciprocal agreements with some international auto clubs (eg Canada's CAA, AA in the UK), so bring your membership card from home.

INSURANCE

California law requires liability insurance for all vehicles. When renting a car, check your home auto-insurance policy or your travel-insurance policy to see if rental cars are already covered. If not, expect to pay about $20 per day for liability insurance when renting a car.

Insurance against damage to the car itself, called Collision Damage Waiver (CDW) or Loss Damage Waiver (LDW), costs another $20 per day for rental cars. The deductible may require you to pay up to the first $500 for any repairs. If you decline CDW, you will be held liable for all damages up to the full value of the car.

Some credit cards cover CDW/LDW, provided you charge the entire cost of the car rental to that card. If you have an accident, you may have to pay the rental-car company first, then seek reimbursement. Most credit-card coverage isn't valid for rentals over 15 days or for 'exotic' models (eg convertibles, 4WD Jeeps).

RENTAL VEHICLES

To rent your own wheels, you'll typically need to be at least 25 years old, hold a valid driver's license and have a major credit card, *not* a check or debit card.

Road Distances (miles)

	Anaheim	Arcata	Bakersfield	Death Valley	Las Vegas	Los Angeles	Monterey	Napa	Palm Springs	Redding	Sacramento	San Diego	San Francisco	San Luis Obispo	Santa Barbara	Sth Lake Tahoe
Arcata	680															
Bakersfield	135	555														
Death Valley	285	705	235													
Las Vegas	265	840	285	140												
Los Angeles	25	650	110	290	270											
Monterey	370	395	250	495	535	345										
Napa	425	265	300	545	590	400	150									
Palm Springs	95	760	220	300	280	110	450	505								
Redding	570	140	440	565	725	545	315	190	650							
Sacramento	410	300	280	435	565	385	185	60	490	160						
San Diego	95	770	230	350	330	120	465	520	140	665	505					
San Francisco	405	280	285	530	570	380	120	50	490	215	85	500				
San Luis Obispo	225	505	120	365	405	200	145	265	310	430	290	320	230			
Santa Barbara	120	610	145	350	360	95	250	370	205	535	395	215	335	105		
Sth Lake Tahoe	505	400	375	345	460	480	285	160	485	260	100	600	185	390	495	
Yosemite	335	465	200	300	415	310	200	190	415	325	160	430	190	230	345	190

Rates generally include unlimited mileage, but expect surcharges for additional drivers and one-way rentals. Airport locations may have cheaper rates but higher fees; if you get a fly-drive package, local taxes may be extra when you pick up the car. Child or infant safety seats are compulsory; reserve them when booking your car.

Major car-rental companies:

Alamo (www.alamo.com)

Avis (www.avis.com)

Budget (www.budget.com)

Dollar (www.dollar.com)

Enterprise (www.enterprise.com)

Fox (www.foxrentacar.com)

Hertz (www.hertz.com)

National (www.nationalcar.com)

Thrifty (www.thrifty.com)

Some major car-rental companies offer 'green' fleets of hybrid or biofuel rental cars, but they're in short supply; make reservations far in advance and expect to pay significantly more for these models. Many companies rent hand-controlled vehicles and vans with wheelchair lifts at no extra charge, but you must also reserve these well in advance.

For independent car rentals, check:

Simply Hybrid (www.simplyhybrid.com) Hybrid car rentals in LA.

Zipcar (www.zipcar.com) Car-sharing club with two dozen California locations.

Car Rental Express (www.carrental express.com) Search for independent car-rental agencies.

Rent-a-Wreck (www.rentawreck.com) Rents to younger drivers, mainly in the LA and San Francisco Bay areas.

Super Cheap! Car Rental (www.super cheapcar.com) Rents to younger drivers in LA, Orange County and San Francisco Bay Area.

Wheelchair Getaways (www.wheelchair getaways.com) Rents wheelchair-accessible vans in San Francisco, LA and San Diego.

Motorcycles

Motorcycle rentals and insurance are very expensive. Discounts may be available for three-day and weekly rentals.

Eagle Rider (www.eaglerider.com) Nationwide compnay with 10 locations in California.

Dubbelju Motorcycle Rentals (www.dubbelju.com; 689a Bryant St, San Francisco)

Route 66 (www.route66riders.com) Harley Davidson rentals in LA's South Bay.

Recreational Vehicles & Campervans

Book Recreational Vehicle (RV) and campervan rentals as far in advance as possible. Rental costs vary by size and model; rates often don't include mileage, bedding or kitchen kits, vehicle prep or taxes. Pets are sometimes allowed (surcharge may apply).

Cruise America (www.cruiseamerica.com) Over 20 RV-rental locations statewide.

El Monte (www.elmonterv.com) Has 15 locations across California and offers AAA discounts.

Happy Travel Campers (www.camperusa.com) Rentals in San Francisco and LA.

Vintage Surfari Wagons (www.vwsurfari.com) LA-based rentals.

BORDER CROSSING

California is an important agricultural state. To prevent the spread of pests and diseases, certain food items (including meats, fresh fruit and vegetables) may not be brought into the state. Bakery items and hard-cured cheeses are admissible. If you drive across the border from Mexico or the neighboring states of Oregon, Nevada or Arizona, you may have to stop for a quick agricultural inspection.

If you're driving across the Mexican border, check the ever-changing passport and visa requirements with the **US Department of State** (http://travel.state.gov) beforehand. **US Customs & Border Protection** (http://apps.cbp.gov/bwt) tracks current wait times at every border crossing. Between San Diego and Tijuana, Mexico, San Ysidro is the world's busiest border crossing. US citizens do not require a visa for stays in Mexico of 72 hours or less within Baja California's border zone.

Unless you're planning an extended stay in Tijuana, taking a car across the Mexican border is more trouble than it's worth. Instead, ride the trolley from San Diego or leave your car on the US side of the border and walk across. If you drive across, you must buy Mexican car insurance either beforehand or at the border crossing.

MAPS

Visitor centers and tourist information offices distribute free (but often very basic) maps. GPS navigation cannot be entirely relied upon, especially in remote desert or mountain areas. If you are planning on doing a lot of driving, you'll need a more detailed road map or atlas. Benchmark Maps' comprehensive *California Road & Recreation Atlas* ($25) is the gold standard, showing campgrounds, recreational areas and topographical land features, although it's less useful for navigating congested urban areas. Members of the American Automobile Association (AAA) or its international affiliates can pick up free driving maps from any of AAA's California offices.

ROAD HAZARDS & CONDITIONS

For highway conditions, including road closures and construction updates, dial ☎800-427-7623 or visit www.dot.ca.gov.

In places where winter driving is an issue, snow tires and tire chains may be required, especially on mountain highways. Ideally, carry your own chains and learn how to use them before you hit the road. Otherwise, chains can usually be bought (but not cheaply) on the highway, at gas stations or in nearby towns. Most car-rental companies don't permit the use of chains. Driving off-road, or on unpaved roads, is also prohibited by most car-rental companies.

In rural areas, livestock sometimes graze next to unfenced roads. These areas are typically signed as 'Open Range,' with the silhouette of a steer. Where deer or other wild animals frequently appear roadside, you'll see signs with the silhouette of a leaping deer. Take these signs seriously, particularly at night or in the fog.

In coastal areas, thick fog may impede driving – slow down and if it's too soupy, get off the road. Along coastal cliffs and on twisting mountain roads, watch out for falling rocks, mudslides and snow avalanches that could damage or disable your car if struck.

ROAD RULES

➡ Drive on the right-hand side of the road.

➡ Talking or texting on a cell (mobile) phone while driving is illegal.

➡ The use of seat belts is required for drivers, front-seat passengers and children under 16.

➡ Infant and child safety seats are required for children under eight years old unless they are at least 4ft 9in tall.

➡ High-occupancy vehicle (HOV) lanes marked with a diamond symbol are reserved for cars with multiple occupants, sometimes only during rush hours.

➡ Unless otherwise posted, the speed limit is 65mph on freeways, 55mph on two-lane undivided highways, 35mph on major city streets and 25mph in business and residential districts.

➡ At intersections, U-turns are permitted unless otherwise posted.

➡ Except where indicated, turning right at red lights after coming to a full stop is permitted, although intersecting traffic still has the right of way.

➡ At four-way stop signs, cars proceed in the order in which they arrived. If two cars arrive simultaneously, the one on the right has the right of way. When in doubt, wave the other driver ahead.

➡ When emergency vehicles (such as police, fire or ambulance) approach from either direction, be sure to carefully pull over to the side of the road.

➡ If a police car is pulled off on the shoulder of the road, drivers in the right-hand lane are

Driving Problem-Buster

What should I do if my car breaks down? Call the roadside emergency assistance number of your car-rental company or, if you're driving your own car, your automobile association. Otherwise, call information (☎411) for the number of the nearest towing service or auto-repair shop.

What if I have an accident? If it's safe to do so, pull over to the side of the road. For minor fender benders with no injuries or significant property damage, exchange insurance information with the other driver and file a report with your insurance provider as soon as possible. For major accidents, call ☎911 and wait for the police and emergency services to arrive.

What should I do if I am stopped by the police? If you are stopped by the police, be courteous. Don't get out of the car unless asked. Keep your hands where the officer can see them (eg on the steering wheel). For traffic violations, there is usually a 30-day period to pay a fine; most matters can be handled by mail. Police can legally give roadside sobriety checks to assess if you've been drinking or using drugs.

What should I do if my car gets towed? Call the police nonemergency number for the town or city that you're in and ask where to pick up your car. Towing and hourly (or daily) storage fees can quickly total hundreds of dollars.

What if I can't find anywhere to stay? If you're traveling during summer and/or holiday periods, always book accommodations in advance, as beds fill up fast. If you're stuck and it's getting late, it's best not to keep driving on aimlessly – just pull into one of those ubiquitous roadside chain motels or hotels.

California Playlist

Surfer Girl Beach Boys

(Sittin' On) The Dock of the Bay Otis Redding

California Love 2Pac & Dr Dre

California Dreamin' The Mamas & the Papas

California Phantom Planet

California Gurls Katy Perry featuring Snoop Dogg

legally required to merge left, as long as it's safe to do so.

➡ It's illegal to carry open containers of alcohol inside a vehicle, even empty ones. Unless containers are full and still sealed, store them in the trunk.

➡ California has strict anti-littering laws; throwing trash from a vehicle may incur a $1000 fine.

PARKING

Parking is plentiful and free in small towns and rural areas, but is generally scarce and expensive in big cities. You can pay municipal parking meters and centralized pay stations with coins (eg quarters) or sometimes credit or debit cards. When parking on the street, read all posted regulations and restrictions (eg street-cleaning hours, permit-only residential areas) and pay attention to colored curbs, or you may be ticketed and towed. Expect to pay at least $2.50 per hour or $25 overnight at a city parking garage. Flat-fee valet parking at hotels and restaurants is common in cities; make sure you tip the valet attendant at least $2 when your keys are handed back to you.

FUEL

➡ Gas stations in California, nearly all of which are self-service, are everywhere, except in national parks and remote desert and mountain areas.

➡ Gas is sold in gallons (one US gallon equals 3.78L). At the time of research, the cost for midgrade fuel was more than $4.

ROAD TRIP WEBSITES

Driving Conditions & Traffic

California Department of Transportation (www.dot.ca.gov) Highway conditions, construction updates and road closures.

511.org (www.511.org) San Francisco Bay Area traffic updates.

go511.com (www.go511.com) LA and Southern California traffic updates.

Automobile Clubs

American Automobile Association (www.aaa.com) Emergency roadside assistance (24-hour), free maps and travel discounts for members.

Better World Club (www.betterworldclub. com) Ecofriendly auto-club alternative to AAA.

Maps

Google Maps (http://maps.google.com) Free online maps and driving directions.

National Park Service (www.nps.gov/ state/ca/index.htm) Links to individual park sites for road condition updates and free downloadable PDF maps.

Road Rules

California Department of Motor Vehicles (www.dmv.ca.gov) Statewide driving laws, driver's licenses and vehicle registration.

BEHIND THE SCENES

SEND US YOUR FEEDBACK

We love to hear from travelers – your comments help make our books better. We read every word, and we guarantee that your feedback goes straight to the authors. Visit **lonelyplanet. com/contact** to submit your updates and suggestions.

Note: We may edit, reproduce and incorporate your comments in Lonely Planet products such as guidebooks, websites and digital products, so let us know if you don't want your comments reproduced or your name acknowledged. For a copy of our privacy policy visit lonelyplanet.com/privacy.

ACKNOWLEDGMENTS

Climate map data adapted from Peel MC, Finlayson BL & McMahon TA (2007) 'Updated World Map of the Köppen-Geiger Climate Classification', *Hydrology and Earth System Sciences*, 11, 163344.

Cover photographs: Front: Bixby Bridge, Michele Falzone/AWL; Back: Julia Pfeiffer Burns State Park, Michele Falzone/AWL

Illustration pp56-7 by Michael Weldon

THIS BOOK

This 1st edition of *Pacific Coast Highways Road Trips* was researched and written by Andrew Bender, Sara Benson, Alison Bing, Celeste Brash, Nate Cavalieri and Adam Skolnick. This guidebook was produced by the following:

Product Editor Katie O'Connell

Senior Cartographer Alison Lyall

Book Designer Katherine Marsh

Assisting Book Designer Cam Ashley

Cover Researcher Campbell McKenzie

Thanks to Shahara Ahmed, Sasha Baskett, Brendan Dempsey, James Hardy, Darren O'Connell, Martine Power, Wibowo Rusli, Luna Soo, Angela Tinson, Clifton Wilkinson

OUR STORY

A beat-up old car, a few dollars in the pocket and a sense of adventure. In 1972 that's all Tony and Maureen Wheeler needed for the trip of a lifetime – across Europe and Asia overland to Australia. It took several months, and at the end – broke but inspired – they sat at their kitchen table writing and stapling together their first travel guide, *Across Asia on the Cheap*. Within a week they'd sold 1500 copies. Lonely Planet was born.

Today, Lonely Planet has offices in Melbourne, London and Oakland, with more than 600 staff and writers. We share Tony's belief that 'a great guidebook should do three things: inform, educate and amuse'.

INDEX